Praise for My Life Encapsulated . . .

Ken's self proclaimed "calling" is to inspire everyone he meets to live on purpose, that we might have the necessary energy required to turn our setbacks into comebacks, turn our stumbling blocks into stepping stones, and validate that if we do today what others won't, we can accomplish tomorrow what others can't.

— DAN CLARK, AUTHOR AND SPEAKER

This remarkable book tells the inspirational, instructional story of one of America's best kept secrets—Ken Brailsford, a quiet business giant who has accomplished much and learned even more. What a blessing that he has written this book so we can see through his eyes and, with a little luck, stand on his shoulders.

— MITCH DAVIS, MOTION PICTURE DIRECTOR

Ken Brailsford came to me with a desire to finish his memoir, always a daunting task for any individual. But as I have worked closely with him and met all of the wonderful people who have contributed to this book, I have literally seen what Ken calls "the invisible hand of God" as it has opened door after door for this to be accomplished. Some say miracles never cease . . . with Ken, this is so true.

— KAREN K. CHRISTOFFERSEN, PRODUCER

My Life
Encapsulated

My Life
Encapsulated

The Path to Success

KEN BRAILSFORD

BookWise
publishing

My Life Encapsulated: The Path to Success by Ken Brailsford

Copyright © 2015 by Ken Brailsford

All rights reserved.

The names of a few individuals in the stories contained in this book have been altered to protect their privacy.

BookWise Publishing
www.bookwisepublishing.com

For additional copies of the book, go to www.kenbrailsford.com.

Interior book design: Eden Graphics, Inc. www.edengraphics.net

Cover photo by Brent Rowland.

Library of Congress Control Number: 2015952523

ISBN 978-1-60645-136-6 Hard Cover
ISBN 978-1-60645-137-3 e Book

10 9 8 7 6 5 4 3 2 1

First Printing

PRINTED IN THE UNITED STATES OF AMERICA

Dedication

For my wife, Linda, and our children,
Kenny, Sheri, John, Lisa, Becky, and Steven

ACKNOWLEDGMENTS

Writing a book is not an easy task, certainly not for me. I've contemplated writing a book—an autobiography—for years and actually started one a couple of years ago. Before I started writing, though, I posted on Facebook to my five thousand followers to find out if they thought it was a good idea. Much to my surprise over a thousand responded in the positive before I couldn't count any longer. That is what began my journey of writing my autobiography. However, it was a daunting task, and the writing soon bogged down as I found it hard to find the time and, yes, sometimes, the motivation (motivator) to move on.

But thinking on that and responding to so many that have asked me questions of my beginnings and how I arrived where I am, and where I am going, I always felt that I had just started writing, and I must complete the adventure at some point. In short, I needed help. That help came initially when I heard that my niece, Darci Moss, was looking for another job. She had worked for me before so I knew her strengths and invited her to work for me with my social media push that I was just beginning. She started and then, I was able to hire Casey, her husband to help as well. They have been remarkable in moving my social presence forward. And now they came to my rescue with this book.

Casey introduced me to Karen Christoffersen of BookWise Publishing who has been responsible for more than 150 books being published. This is no small feat, and, as my project manager, she has been the guiding light and leader in making this book a reality. She brought my editor, N.C. Allen, an accomplished writer herself, to the table. I am indebted to her also for being able to polish my words, and, yes, in some cases, sounding like me with only the concept of what I wanted said.

Fran Platt of Eden Design joined us to design and layout the book. She has done a remarkable job. That, in and of itself, is what makes a book a book.

Much of my work, and certainly the interviews, were recorded. Casey and Darci did all of the interviews and chose all of the questions they wanted to ask. The interviews, which are an important part of this work, in that I can be seen through the eyes of these individuals, wouldn't have happened without Darci and Casey.

I can't say enough good about Karen. As project manager, she is the one who pushed the timetable, making everything come together. I loved working with Karen, Nancy, Fran, Casey, and Darci. *My Life Encapsulated* never would have seen the light of day without all of them and the long hours it took to make this a reality. Thank you all. I look forward to working with all of you on future projects.

And last, but not least, to my family, both immediate and extended, and to many of my business associates, thank you for your honesty and forthrightness with your unscripted and frank words. These interviews allowed me and so many others to see myself through your eyes. For that I will be eternally grateful.

CONTENTS

ACKNOWLEDGMENTS. IX

FOREWORD XV

INTRODUCTION XXI

CHAPTER 1: *The Invisible Hand of God* 1

CHAPTER 2: *Born of Goodly Parents* 5

CHAPTER 3: *I Want to Know if You Really Exist* 13

CHAPTER 4: *Aunts and Uncles and Cousins* 19

CHAPTER 5: *How Do I Become Something
That I'm Not* 27

CHAPTER 6: *I Never Want to See You Walking* 35

CHAPTER 7: *The Spirit of the Bayonet* 47

CHAPTER 8: *A Second Mission* 57

CHAPTER 9: *I Think I Have Something You'd Be
Interested In* 69

CHAPTER 10: *Spared* 85

CHAPTER 11: *You Saw More in Me Than I Saw
in Myself* 91

CHAPTER 12: *Multi-Tasking at Its Finest* 99

CHAPTER 13: *Lessons Learned*. 107

CHAPTER 14: *The Underdog Dilemma* 115

CHAPTER 15: *What's It All For?* 121

CHAPTER 16: *Some Final Thoughts*. 123

INTERVIEWS: *Amazing People in My Life* 125

Q&A: *Ken & Linda Brailsford* 209

FOREWORD

IN WRITING A FOREWORD for the life and times of this extraordinary man, my interaction with him clearly illuminated five fundamental truths:

- The purpose of a leader is to grow more leaders, by doing an analog job in a digital world;

- Wisdom is the gift of the elderly—which means when an old man dies an entire library burns to the ground (unless of course someone captures his words of wisdom);

- Too many live their lives hoping to be happy, but because they only hope they never really are. They are waiting for someone to invite them to the prom and have never taken the time to learn how to dance;

- You can fail at what you don't want, so you might as well take a chance on doing what you love;

- Successful people get what they want by focusing on a destination that's impressive and matters for the moment. Significant individuals want what they get by focusing on a journey that's important and matters most (which means it lasts the longest), so they don't die with their music still in them.

Yes, this masterpiece is a detailed collection of memories, game-changing events, and monumental moments, both public and private, that a special man experienced, which introduced improved health and wellness, personal and leadership development, financial security, and an elevated life of unlimited opportunities to millions of people worldwide. But most importantly, this book is an insightful look into the mind and motivation that molded this man, and an up close and personal glance at the heart and soul of one of the greatest entrepreneurs of the twenty-first century.

One day I was visiting my friend and associate in his executive office. Suddenly a soft knock came at the door. When he opened it, his face lit up like a Christmas tree. For there standing in the doorway was an immaculate sharp-dressed man in an expensive charcoal gray suit, starched white shirt and blue silk tie who immediately flashed a warm inviting smile that solicited a hugging embrace. Although small in stature, his larger-than-life presence more than filled the room and somehow showcased his character, gentle kindness, and love of life without speaking a word. I instantaneously knew he was someone uniquely special. I was in the presence of greatness.

As we were introduced, I was drawn to his sincere eye contact, impressed by his firm handshake, intrigued by his certain sense of self, and immediately reminded of the story about French King Louis XVI.

When Louis the XVI was forced from his throne and imprisoned, his young son, the prince, was kidnapped by those who overthrew the kingdom. They thought that inasmuch as the king's son was heir to the throne, if they could destroy him morally, he wouldn't realize the great and grand destiny that life had bestowed upon him.

They took him to a community far away and exposed the boy to every filthy and vile thing that life could offer. They exposed him to foods that would quickly make him a slave to appetite, continuously used vulgar language around him, and constantly exposed him to lewd and lusting women, alcohol, gambling, dishonor, and distrust.

For over six months he was bombarded twenty-four hours a day by everything that could drag the soul of a man into wickedness, rude, crude, defiled, and unrefined behavior. But never once did the young prince buckle under pressure. Finally, his captors gave up on tempting and changing him and asked why had he not submitted himself to partaking of these worldly pleasures to satisfy these most lustful desires that were his for the taking.

With a deep and confident sense of self, the boy proudly and humbly answered, "I cannot do what you ask, for I was born to be a king."

No, this extraordinary, sophisticated, elegant, gracious, extremely intelligent, passionate, creative, imaginative, visionary, superstar entrepreneur, whom I met that day in my friend's office, is not, and will never be a king of a castle. However, with this same special sense of who he is and what he was born to be, he is the original "king" and reigning ruler of the concept of "encapsulating" mother earth's plants, herbs, berries, and natural ingredients, which he single-handedly turned into a new multi-billion dollar industry that for over forty years has literally changed the world!

His name is Ken Brailsford: my hero, my mentor, my friend.

As you will discover, it all started when Ken was a young teenager with an experiment boiling, drinking and later selling "chaparral," an herb growing on the side of the highway that proved to be a remedy for his mother's serious health condition, followed by hand-filling bottles of home-made cayenne pepper capsules, which soon caught on as a remedy for ulcers. Two years later, Ken turned his family enterprise into a multi-level marketing company called Nature's Sunshine Products, and as they say, the rest is history, leading to the formation of other extraordinary companies, including Enrich International and Zija International.

Most significantly, Ken is a committed family man (who realizes no other success can compensate for failure in the home), a successful businessman (who realizes 'wealth flows through you, not to you—you can get anything in life you want if you are willing to help enough other people get what they want'), and a deeply devoted faith-based man of God (who realizes we are more than mere mortal beings, living on a small planet, for a short season. We are spiritual beings having a physical experience with the commandment that 'to whom much is given, much is expected.').

Watching how Ken treats others, witnessing his covenant to ethical core values and total trusting business practices, and hearing him share his conviction that 'the invisible hand of God' started him down a path and has continually led him physically, mentally, spiritually, and financially on a step by step journey to make a living and a significant difference, inspires everyone who meets him to follow his example and emulate his greatness.

I appreciate the fact that although he is a highly educated, trained, and experienced businessman, his self proclaimed "calling" is to inspire everyone he meets to live on purpose, that we might have the necessary energy required to turn our setbacks into comebacks, turn our stumbling blocks into stepping stones, and validate that if we do today what others won't, we can accomplish tomorrow what others can't. I love, admire, and honor Ken Brailsford, and when you turn the last page and click off your reading light, you will love, admire, and honor him too!

— DAN CLARK

INTRODUCTION

THIS BOOK IS ABOUT the course of my life, encapsulated, so to speak. But it is not just about me. It is about so many mentioned and unmentioned people who influenced my life for good, starting with my parents and grandparents (and, of course, my wife and children). They left me and, continue to leave me, a legacy to follow, a path that brings happiness and success into my life. They loved me with a god-like love, and it made me want to listen to them, to obey them (most of the time), and taught me to pray, to know God, and especially to love God.

I feel my life has been led by "the invisible hand of God," as I call it. It cannot be seen, but it can be felt, not so much in one's youth and middle age, but later in life. When one looks back after decades of experience, both sad and happy, unsuccessful at times, and successful, one can look through the eyes of those experiences and see God's footprints in the sand, as it were, leading, protecting, loving, encouraging one along the chosen path that He wants us to follow.

Of course, if one is to follow that path, he must be willing to put others before self, he must learn to follow God's ways, and most important, he must be willing to sacrifice his own will and turn it over to God. That is probably the hardest thing a person must do to follow that path. I hope that I have learned to do that, even though deep down I know, at times, I have strayed from that path.

I've certainly tried to follow it. I've always wanted to make my parents proud of me, and what I've done to better the life entrusted to me by God, and my family. I want Him to smile down upon me and my efforts. Someday, I want to return to His presence and be with those that I love—my family and my dear friends and acquaintances. I hope that we can all follow that path.

I've written this book, not by way of bragging, but to answer so many that have asked how I got to where I am and to learn where I'm going. It is certainly easier to explain how I got here than to say where I'm going. Remember, we don't always know where we are going, but it is God's will that decides our path, if we but let Him. Even if we do follow His will, it is definitely hard to tell what the future holds for us anyway. Will we have success or a lack of it, health or sickness, are we leaders or not? Do we have enough money to survive on in these trying days? Do we make excuses for ourselves when we make a mistake? Do we take full responsibility for what we do? Or do we learn from our mistakes and missteps and move on? If we've committed a sin against mankind or God, have we repented, changed our way, and moved on? Do we hold grudges, or do we forgive others? Do we always do our best in everything we do?

These are just some of the questions I ask myself often, but I think the most important question to ask is: *Have we made a positive impact in this world?* When we arrive here, we use oxygen, food, space, time, and so many other things, visible and invisible, and perhaps thousands of people have contributed to our lives, hopefully mostly positive. Have we paid the price for that, or have we just drifted, feeling entitled? Do we expect and let others pay our way in life? I think if this is the case we will be unhappy with ourselves when we get to the other side and can see ourselves the way others see us, especially the way God sees us. I think we will be able to feel their feelings and yes, even God's feelings, at that time. Fortunately, God loves us, we are His children, so I believe, even there we can change and be better, the way He expected and wanted us to be in this life.

So this is my life. At least up to this point. I want and feel that I have so much more to give, both in my MLM company Zija, and my other myriad of businesses and the people that work for me. I love them all, even if I don't know them all—the distributors, employees of Zija and my former MLM companies, the employees of my current companies, past and present, and even those companies that failed. At times I lost money, sometimes a lot, but the employees who lost their jobs probably paid the highest price. To those I am sincerely sorry. I did the best I could, even when that wasn't enough.

I hope you enjoy this journey and can see "the invisible hand of God" in it and, perhaps, identify that Hand in your own lives.

— KEN BRAILSFORD

*I take particular pleasure
in acknowledging that
the interposing hand of Heaven,
in various instances of our preparations
for this operation
has been most conspicuous and remarkable.*

— GEORGE WASHINGTON

My first ride on a real horse . . . and staying on!

CHAPTER 1

The Invisible Hand of God

I DO NOT BELIEVE IN COINCIDENCES. I think things happen for a reason. I believe what I've come to recognize as "the invisible hand of God" in my life; I believe that God places things in our lives to take us down a certain path that He's prepared us for, a path that will be for the benefit of His children. And I think His hand is in everyone's lives, whether we recognize it or not. When you're young and you're looking forward, it's hard to see that invisible hand of God. When you get older, though, and you look back, it becomes easier to see where it's led you, and why. Sometimes you fall off the horse and need some help getting back on, and staying on!

I was a young man with a wife and two children when I finished a stint in the military, and, when that was done, I needed a job. My wife and I had a family gathering with several of her aunts and uncles who lived near us at the time. Together, we all decided to start a family business. We decided we'd each contribute $150—none of us had very much money—and we came up with a grand total of $1050. Great!

We quickly realized, however, that every idea we came up with was going to cost a lot more than that, just in start-up costs alone, and none of us had any more money to put into it. So as we scratched our heads, my wife's aunt, Kristine, said, "Why don't we put cayenne pepper in a capsule?"

Everybody turned to her, wondering why in the world we would ever do that. To me, it sounded like the craziest thing anyone had ever said. So she explained. A few years earlier, her husband, Gene, had surgery for bleeding ulcers. Upon his release from the hospital, his doctor told him he'd see him back in a few years for additional surgery.

Poor Gene went home so depressed. He thought the surgery had cured him, so he was disappointed at the thought of future surgeries, and he moped around his house feeling sorry for himself. A neighbor came over to check on his recovery and asked him about his long face. When Gene related the doctor's pessimistic prediction, she said, "There's an easy solution for that, Gene. Take a teaspoon of cayenne pepper and chug it down with a glass of water every day. You'll never have trouble with stomach ulcers again."

Have you ever tried that? Uncle Gene must have been desperate because he did just that for several years. And amazingly enough, he never had another bleeding ulcer. Apparently, though, cayenne pepper is not an easy thing to swallow. While soothing for the stomach, it burns like

> God places things in our lives to take us down a certain path that He's prepared us for.

fire in the mouth. As Kristine finished telling her story to us, she said, "I'd rather die than do what Gene did. So that's why we should put it in capsules."

So we all thought, *Why not?* It was worth a try. We bought three pounds of cayenne pepper powder, 3,000 gelatin capsules, and 30 plastic bottles. We sat around a big, round table in their kitch-

> I think His hand is in everyone's life, whether we recognize it or not.

en and, as a family, stuffed those capsules full of that pepper until we had 3,000 capsules full, 30 bottles worth. Do you know how hard that is to do when your eyes are watering and your nose running, your hands are stained red, and you're thinking you must be crazy?

I'll tell you right now, it was a miserable experience. But we had our product. And what followed was a journey that has taken me places I'd never imagined as a young boy, growing up in good but humble circumstances, with good and humble people. And as I've looked back on my life, I can see threads of certain values that have woven together to create the person I've become, and I've seen that invisible hand of God, guiding me along, sometimes pulling me back, keeping me in the saddle, to set me on this amazing path.

Me with my parents in Niagara Falls, New York 1944

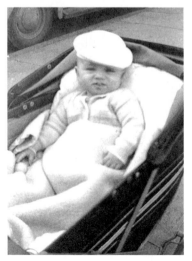

Early 1945 . . . I'm about four months old

CHAPTER 2

Born of Goodly Parents . . .

I was an only child, born to Robert and Freeda Brailsford on September 23, 1944, when they lived in Niagara Falls, New York. My dad was a research scientist working for the Hooker Chemical Company on the Manhattan Project. It was so secret and compartmentalized at the time that I'm not sure he even knew what he was working on.

Dad told me once about an explosion at the plant. At first it was assumed that the Nazis had been behind it and the FBI conducted a thorough investigation. It was later determined that it had been nothing more than an accident, but it had been fairly harrowing for my father. He had been close enough that all of his hair was singed, but he was otherwise unhurt.

The war effort reached everyone in those days. My mother was a fighter plane line inspector at the Bell Aircraft factory in Buffalo, New York and worked until just a few days before my birth. She began on the assembly line but became an inspector who, along with her boss, did the final inspections of all the systems associated with the aircraft. She loved her work and excelled at it. She soon found herself with the title of "Inspector." She had the "stamp." She and her boss were the only two in that factory who could stamp off and approve every system on the fighter planes, determining they were built correctly and could be sent off to Europe for combat.

The factory had a policy that at seven months pregnant, women weren't allowed to work any longer. I was her second and only successful pregnancy and she hid it from her boss as best she could. Knowing my mother, she probably didn't reveal her condition to any other coworkers, either. My parents needed her wages and she wanted to work right up until delivery.

As the pregnancy advanced, her boss figured it out, but he never said anything to her because she was too valuable. After all, only the two of them could inspect and stamp approval on the fighters as they came off the assembly line. He was under extreme pressure to produce more aircraft and he needed her. As she neared seven months, she became bold with her boss. She had a way of joking and yet being serious at the same time. She told him she was quitting unless he gave her a raise. And she did this more than once. It was a bluff but it always worked. She got her raises every time.

I have a stubborn streak which I believe I inherited from my mother. A defective plane came off of the line once and she inspected it. She spotted the defect and refused to stamp the papers. My impression is that they must have been on a short leash for aircraft that month because her boss demanded that she release the fighter. But she was strong, stubborn, and unwavering in her sense of right and wrong. She refused and handed the papers back to her boss, telling him, "You have a stamp, you stamp it. I will not be responsible for a young American pilot's death." She walked away and left him standing there open-mouthed, suspecting she'd be fired immediately. He didn't fire her and I never did find out what happened with that plane. All I know is that my mom wouldn't release it.

Mom finished her shift each night close to midnight and then had to walk two or three miles to catch a bus home, which was about twenty miles away. Rain, shine, snow, she never missed work. One night on her way to the bus station in a heavy snow-storm, a fellow male worker drove by and stopped, offering her ride in exchange for sex. She "strongly declined." And knowing my mom, I'm sure the man was on the receiving end of an extremely stern lecture.

I have a stubborn streak and I believe I inherited it from my mother.

My paternal grandfather's name was John Henry Brailsford. He had offered his diamond ring to the first grandchild named after him. It could have been me! Coincidently, the doctor who delivered me was also named John Henry, and when I was born, he asked Mom what my name would be. Her response was, "For sure, not John Henry," and the poor doctor was stunned, thinking she meant him.

My mother knew her mind, knew who she was, and what she wanted, diamond ring for her son or not. After I was born, her job became me. She did return to the work force at various times during my life, but I was the main beneficiary of her focus and attention. I think I got my Type A traits from her. She was a natural leader. Her strength and unflagging work ethic, as well as that of my good father, were examples to me of how to live life, examples that I've drawn from consistently.

> Mother was a natural leader. Her strength and unflagging work ethic, as well as that of my good father, were examples to me of how to live life.

My earliest recollections of life are of our rented apartment in Provo, Utah when I was roughly three or four. I think my love for entertaining a crowd established itself fairly early on. I remember dancing as a very small boy for some visitors to the home and, of course, when everyone laughed it only encouraged the behavior more.

My father was quiet and reserved. Much of my early personality resembled his. He was an effective parent in that he certainly *didn't* have to say much. The only spanking I remember in my life wasn't severe, in fact I figured that I'd better cry so he wouldn't continue with it, even though I didn't feel like I needed to cry.

I remember one other time I saw him get upset. It was because they put me to bed and I didn't stay there. Remember I was an only child, so I didn't have the example of siblings to follow after, which meant I blazed my own trail. And this one particular night, I'd gotten up several times and Dad kept putting me back to bed. The last time I got up, I saw him getting angry, so I quickly went back to my room. I learned it was just better for me to stay in bed when my parents put me there. All things considered, I think I was a fairly easy child.

I've been told I loved to dance!

In those early days, I remember walking across the street and holding my dad's hand as we crossed when I said, "Can you buy me a five-cent candy bar?" And his response was no, that we couldn't afford it. I remember that as clear as yesterday. I never asked my parents for money the rest of my life because of that one comment. I wasn't upset that we couldn't afford it, but at the time it taught me I had to stand up and provide for myself. I knew if I wanted a candy bar, I wanted to be able to buy it myself.

Threads of the personal health code I live by in my life

began in those early years. I recall finding a cigarette butt in the gutter outside our home. I thought I was mister macho man, picked it up, and pretended to smoke. My dad saw me, immediately removed it from my lips, and disgustedly threw it away. This wasn't my only attempt at pretending to smoke. When I was older, I bought a box of candy cigarettes. That lasted only until Dad caught me again. His clear disgust made an impression on me. In those days, the Marlboro Man was very popular on billboards. Other tobacco companies had their advertisements, too; but my father's disapproval was always very apparent. Given my beginnings, it's little wonder

Here I am loving my ice cream cone in Provo, Utah.
(Ice cream was just as important as a candy bar!)

I've found myself involved in businesses whose aim is to help people be healthy.

Perhaps my father understood on some level that life itself could be a fragile thing. It was around this time that my dad walked across State Street in Orem one night and was hit by a car. He was hurt very seriously and could have been killed. I was asleep when all this happened. I remember getting up in the night and seeing the bathtub full of bloody clothes. I asked my mom about it and she said, "Oh, that was just an old bum that got hit by a car and I'm washing his clothes." My mother was that way, she tried to lighten things up any time she could. I think, like many mothers, she wanted to shield me from painful things.

I remember my dad coming home from the hospital a couple days later, his whole head bandaged. His entire scalp had been full of gravel. He was lucky to be alive. I remember seeing that bandage on his head for a long time. I was too young to know the seriousness of it or how close I came to not having a living father. But it was an experience that taught me compassion for people who are injured or hurt.

Looking back on it now, I wonder if that near miss was a precursor for an event that was quite tragic in my young life. I had a dog at that time named Booie. My aunt and uncle found him as a stray out on the highway while visiting California. When they came back to Utah, they gave me Booie. He was a faithful companion for a long time until he was hit on that same street, State Street, and didn't live. Being an only child, that dog meant a lot to me. He was always with me before and after school—any time I was home.

I remember waking up one night and no one was home. I didn't know where my parents were. It must have been about midnight. I didn't know what to do—I was scared. So I sat on the couch looking out the window, hoping and watching for my parents. They finally came home and put me back to bed. It was only years later I found out Dad would walk to the corner and wait for the midnight bus that would bring my mother home from work.

At that time, she worked at the State Mental Hospital where they housed all of the mentally insane. My mother was tough. Firm. She'd been trained to never let anyone out of the locked facility, no matter who they said they were. Many inmates had grandiose ideas; some of them thought they were Napoleon or President of the United States. You name it, someone imagined it.

One evening there was a woman banging on the door saying, "I need to get out, I'm Dr. So and So's wife!" The doctor was the head of the whole mental institution, of course. My mother said to her, "Oh yeah, I'm sure you are," and wouldn't let her out. It turned out later, my mother found out that woman really was the doctor's wife! She'd gone in there just to look around and didn't get back out until someone finally rescued her. But it wasn't my mother! Mom hadn't seen her before and because she'd been trained not to believe anything she was told, she didn't.

My parents were consistent and fair, two lessons I learned early on in life that remain with me always.

CHAPTER 3

I Want to Know if You Really Exist . . .

I HAVE A VERY VIVID MEMORY of a particular incident when we lived near Liberty Park in Salt Lake City. My mother wouldn't let me do something so I stuck my tongue out at her. Before I could say or do anything, her hand came out and hit the bottom of my chin so hard I bit my tongue. Boy, it hurt! But more than the physical pain, my pride was hurt. I turned around and said "I'm going to run away."

I left the house and walked down the street, looking back to see if Mom was coming. I thought for sure she'd come after me and rescue me. But my mother was not a rescuer; neither was my father, even considering how young I was then.

I walked a little farther, looked around, and nobody came! Then I walked the whole block and looked around. Nothing. So I decided I was going to walk to my grandparents' house. They lived in downtown Salt Lake, about three miles away, and to a little kid, that was a very long way. I didn't get more than a couple of blocks. When I saw nobody was

> I have to know if there is a God. And if there is not a God, I will never go to church again.

coming, I walked back home with my head hanging down and apologized to my mother. I never stuck my tongue out at her or anyone else ever again. Interestingly enough, that's one thing I won't tolerate from my children either.

My childhood was really quite idyllic and full of the kind of play you don't see as the norm these days with kids. We had no video games to occupy our time, no Internet, no cell phones, no social media. I played War with marbles or little plastic characters. I loved that game of War, and I played both sides, but one side was always "me" and, of course, it was the hero side. I'd play it on our wooden floor for hours at a time, learning strategies and just pretending. Life itself created patterns that enabled me to put my natural talents to good practice for strengthening the traits I would later need in business.

A certain amount of independence asserted itself into my life while I was still in elementary school. My father went back to college at the University of Utah to earn a PhD in metallurgy and organic chemistry. My mother worked at the ZCMI credit department to support the family. I often visited her there after school. Her parents lived just a couple of blocks away. So my geographical world at that time was contained to a fairly small radius and I was able to walk just about everywhere I needed to go. I often went to my grandparents' home after school and my grandmother would make me peanut butter and honey sandwiches. I'd have my snack with them, then walk the couple of blocks to my house and play, finding things in the house to use for my own made-up games.

Once I was a little older, every Saturday my parents gave me thirty cents and let me walk a few blocks to downtown. I would pass Temple Square, walking on the ledge of the wall around the temple as only little kids will sometimes do. I walked to every theater downtown to determine which movie I would see. I paid the twenty-five cent admission, buying a five-cent box of Dots, my favorite candy. I would watch the movie, usually a double-feature, and it was wonderful. Sometimes it was a serial movie with Buck Rogers flying through space on rockets. I loved those kinds of shows.

I remember one time my parents wanted me to see *The Robe*, a movie about Jesus, starring Kirk Douglas. It sounded boring to me. Sure enough, when I looked at the billboard outside the theater, it looked boring—so I went to *King Kong* instead. I think my parents were a little disappointed when I told them I saw *King Kong* instead of a movie about the Savior, but what was a young boy who loved action movies to do? Looking back, I wonder if I didn't want to see *The Robe* because it had been suggested to me. I wanted to be independent and be my own boss even at that age.

I remember those Saturdays with such a sense of nostalgia. It was wonderful to be able to go about all by myself in a day and age when a young boy could walk the streets of a big city and never worry about being harmed or molested. I was, in fact, still very young. One of my Saturday movie excursions was to see the movie *Superman*. I decided that if Superman could fly, I could put on a cape and fly off our third story balcony. I got a towel and a safety pin, put my cape around my neck, and stood out on that balcony fully determined to jump off and fly. A little apprehensive, I was getting ready to leap just as my parents came home. It was my mother who caught me and saved me. That was one of many times God has intervened and saved my life. Always, I've seen His intervention saving me from my own stupidity at times.

My best friend was Gerald Cunningham. Behind his house was a large, vacant field. Every summer he and I and many other boys played baseball. I became proficient in any position I played, which is not to say that I was a great baseball player. But I thought I was! And I never struck out. It was a simpler era and we had a great time. Sometimes we'd vary the routine and do something else. We'd use cinder blocks and lay them out into what I'd mapped out in my mind as a city. We piled some two-by-eights on top of the blocks and had quite an empire. We created our own games, entertaining ourselves all day long until the sun went down.

Despite the fact that I chose to see *King Kong* over *The Robe*, I really was a curious boy when it came to bigger questions about spirituality and whether or not God actually existed. My first truly spiritual experience came one Sunday when a Sunday school teacher shared a story that made an impact on me. It struck so deep in my soul that I left Sunday school and was walking home, pondering this story. I remember thinking, "I have to know if there is a God. And if there is not a God, I will never go to church again." I was determined as only a young boy *can* be determined.

I walked home, found myself alone in the apartment

where my parents and I lived, and I was working up a plan to figure how I could find out about the existence of God so I would have irrefutable proof one way or the other. I finally determined I would take a half-sheet of paper, put it on the dresser that was in the bedroom, and place a pencil there, which I did. Then I would pray and tell God it was up to Him.

I remember kneeling by the side of my bed and saying, "Heavenly Father, if You really exist, I expect You to sign that piece of paper. I don't need to see You sign it, I will give You privacy, but when I come back in, if there's no signature, I will know You do not exist, and I will never go to church again for my whole life."

I was fully determined. I got up from that prayer, walked into the kitchen, having shut the door to the bedroom behind me as I wanted to give God His privacy, and then I thought *how long will it take Him? I think five minutes will do.* Above our small table there was a clock hanging on the wall. I watched the second-hand go around five times, ever so slowly. It seemed like it would never end. When the five minutes were over, I very reverently walked across the hall, cautiously opened the door, and slid into the room.

From that day forward, I never doubted the existence of God.

What I experienced was nothing less than miraculous. I felt God in that room to the very last cell and fiber in my body, so much so that I said immediately, "I don't want to see You!" I was afraid to see God. I was just a little boy. I didn't know what that would mean, but I didn't want to see Him.

I didn't even bother looking at that piece of paper, at least not at that point, because I knew that God lived. He was in that room with me! Although I didn't see Him, I knew He was there. That was all the proof I needed. From that day forward, I never doubted the existence of God and what He expected and wanted of me as a boy.

From then on, I had no problems going to church.

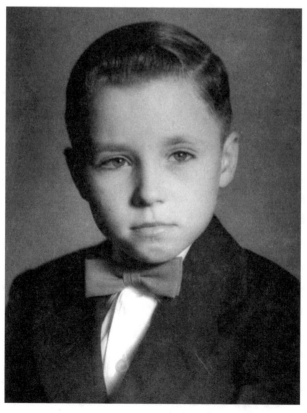

Even when I was very young, I was seriously contemplating God's existence.

CHAPTER 4

Aunts and Uncles and Cousins...

EXTENDED FAMILY WAS QUITE A SIGNIFICANT part of my life when I was young. When my father completed his PhD in Salt Lake City, we moved to Cedar City, Utah where he took a position teaching at the college there. We lived in a small, two-bedroom home that was heated with a coal furnace. It was dirty and dusty and sooty, and sometimes I had to help clean the clinkers out—what a filthy, messy job!

My Aunt Ramona and Uncle Joe lived on the other side of town and, for whatever reason, my parents put me in *their* neighborhood school. So during school I'd have friends over there, and after school and on weekends, I had friends where we lived. Our church was just across the street, with the college and laboratory where my dad taught only a block away, so everything was easy to get to. I rode bicycles a lot.

I had a friend around the corner and down south about a block named Robert Wasden. We were best friends. In the summer his parents put a mattress outside for us to throw our sleeping bags on so we could sleep outside. So many times we'd look up at the stars and talk about the beauty of the sky, the magnificence of it. I'm sure that played a role later in my life as I contemplated God's creations and how in terms of everything we are so small.

My mother, Freeda, me (about nine years old), and my dad, Robert

I had a cousin, David, whose parents were the aunt and uncle who had given me Booie. David was eight years younger than me and he really became the little brother I'd never had but always wanted. I got to see him often, at least every summer. I remember teaching David how to play chess when he was about four years old, not because I wanted to make him a great player, but because I was a poor player—and I wanted to win!

One particular time in Cedar City, David had come to spend the summer with us. We went out into the field behind my house and climbed over a barbed wire fence. I don't remember what our plans were when we got over the barbed wire, but as David started to come over the fence, he fell and his arm was stuck on one of the barbs. (Remember, he was only four.) It caused him to bleed profusely. So I had to lift him off of that nasty fence and take him home with a bloody arm. He went to the ER and had to have some stitches.

On another occasion, David and I were looking at my brand new .22 caliber rifle. I had been taught how to always check and make sure the gun was unloaded after I used it. This particular afternoon, I was aiming the gun toward the window and preparing to dry shoot it. I had it cocked and ready to fire, and just then David moved and was standing with the barrel pointed right at him. I heard two different voices in my head, seemingly yelling in each ear—one telling me to pull the trigger and the other telling me not to. I opted to listen to the one saying not to pull the trigger. I released the hammer slowly, pointed the gun at the floor and pumped the .22. A bullet flipped out of the chamber. I realized how close I came to shooting my cousin and thanked God for prompting me not to pull the trigger.

We played a lot of business games together and this is where I can see the seeds of my love for business take root. I invented a business game and cut out newspaper for play money. A couple other kids came over and we'd walk around the basement setting up stores and buying products from one store to sell to another. I thought a lot about these sorts of things, and since I couldn't make real money, I made my own.

In the fifth grade, my mind was always working, conjuring up different things to do. A lot of things held my interest in those years. I decided I was going to start an army. I knew all the ranks from five-star general to private and I decided I was going to have one person in each rank. Of course, I would be the five-star general. So I went around the school, beginning with my own class, and soon had a full army. Everyone did everything I told them to do, for a few days anyway, until we disbanded.

Of course I would be the five-star general.

Also in fifth grade, there was a kid in the class who picked on me continually. He was a tall and skinny; I was short. And there was another bully in the class who tried to pick on me. I just tried to be their friend and they probably thought that made me weak. One day the tall, skinny kid had a sharpened pencil that he was pointing at me, chiding and calling me a sissy. It accidentally slipped and poked me in the cheek. It didn't hurt a lot, but it drew blood.

That was it. It set me off. I said, "Okay, I'm going to fight you after school. I'll meet you then." And that's not me! I really don't like to fight. But despite my size, I've always been quite physically strong, although I didn't know it at the time. I just knew I was really angry.

In addition to my strength, I had the benefit of fury on my side. I threw him down to the gravel driveway, got on top of him and pushed his face sideways into the gravel so his cheek was mashed into it. He made the mistake of kicking his feet, trying to free himself from me, and did a 360 degree turn, the gravel digging even deeper into his face. When we got through, all this skin was scraped off the side of his face.

I let him up. He went his way and I went mine. He didn't bother me anymore and actually became a good friend after that. The one other bully in the class stopped bothering me as well. So I learned that sometimes you have to defend yourself. You get to that point. I've never had to fight anyone since. I generally have learned how to get along with even my worst enemies, to become friends so they respect me enough to not bother me. That's what you do as a smaller person, as a rule, and we're all smaller at some point than others. But in the fifth grade, it only took once. That reputation stayed with me and it gave me a lot of confidence. I figured even though I was smaller I could beat them up if I had to!

We played games outdoors all the time. Cops and robbers, cowboys and Indians, and I was always the Lone Ranger. We created plays that we performed on my huge front porch. I would script them in my mind and tell everyone what their roles were and the things they should say. My friends, cousins, and I spent entire summers creating our own worlds.

Sometimes we went "window screeching," not one of my prouder moments. We'd walk around at night and put a safety pin into a window screen with a silk thread on it. The idea was to screech that safety pin against the window—it made the weirdest noise—and scare whoever was inside the house. I remember one time a man came after us and almost caught me. It was the last time I ever went window screeching. I didn't like doing things where I would be in trouble. And that was trouble.

My cousin, Jay, was two years older than me and was like

a brother to me. I thought he was a bit mean at times but I enjoyed being around him. His older brother, Fred, was several years older than Jay. He was really almost an adult. I loved my Aunt Ramona and Uncle Joe. Ramona was so kind to me. I could go over there and spend the night anytime I wanted to, as long as it was okay with my mother. They had a screened-in veranda in the back and in the summer it was wonderful to sleep out there in the cool breeze. Jay and I told stories and talked until late in the night.

Joe and Ramona had a daughter, Dorothy, who was three months older than me. When we were about thirteen, Uncle Joe, Aunt Ramona, and my parents decided they were going to go to California. My dad was interviewing for a teaching job in Bakersfield. They figured we were mature enough to be on our own and decided we could tend Max, who wasn't more than two or three, and David, who was only a couple years older than Max. That meant we would be home alone for a couple nights with the little boys.

We had a lot of fun tending them, being very responsible. But we heard on the radio about a prisoner who had escaped from the county jail. So we became a little panicky and nervous. We locked all the doors and windows. Then we found a rusty sword and got my .22 caliber rifle for protection. We were too afraid to sleep in separate bedrooms, so we slept sideways in the bed with Max and David between us. We didn't even put our pajamas on, probably because we were boy and girl, but also we were afraid!

> We had alot of fun, being very responsible.

The prisoner never did show up at my house and we made it through the night okay. Our parents returned home and were very happy with us for doing so well tending the boys. I remember feeling proud. It ended up being a good experience.

CHAPTER 5

How Do I Become Something That I'm Not...

N OT LONG AFTER DOROTHY AND I protected Max and David from the escaped inmate, my father took the teaching position as chemistry professor at the Junior College in Bakersfield, California. I was twelve and we moved there in the heat of the summer. It was 110 degrees the first time I set foot in Bakersfield and witnessed a man passing out on the sidewalk as we were downtown shopping. I wasn't either sad or glad about the move to Bakersfield. I've always looked forward to the next adventure in my life. In fact, by the time I moved to California with my parents, I'd already moved thirteen times, an average of once a year. With that kind of track record, what's one more move? It was just part of life.

Our home in Bakersfield was brand new. In the past we had generally rented, other than the one time in Orem where my dad built the home. I believe this was for a specific reason. My parents never bought "on time." They never borrowed money and they were very frugal. If they didn't have cash, they wouldn't buy.

The new home was on the east side of Bakersfield and it was wonderful. I gave me a good sense of having roots. I started to make friend. Thankfully, I've always been able to do that very quickly. I focused especially on the downtrodden, those who didn't have a lot of friends. I wanted to pick them up and make them happy. They became my friends, not necessarily the popular kids, although I was friends with most of the popular kids, too. But my closest friends were the ones who had typically had a harder time making friends or fitting in.

I started seventh grade at Bakersfield Junior High. It was an uneventful period as school went, but I do remember one experience vividly to this day. Although I didn't realize it at the time, it made a huge impact on me.

As I said, I was small for my age. My parents held me back in the second grade and had me repeat that year because I was so small. I couldn't fit into the third grade desks. I was the kid always at the low end of the growth chart for my age. And even with that one year repeated, I was still on the small side in my classes. There was a big kid in seventh grade who approached me one day and wanted to borrow a quarter. I loaned it to him, privately figuring I wasn't ever going to get it back, even though he said he'd pay me back the next day.

> I thought that in my own way, I'm just as important as anyone else in this life.

The next day came, and much to my surprise, he gave me the money back. Then he immediately asked to borrow another quarter with the same "I'll pay you back tomorrow" promise. Like a fool, I gave it to him. I think I was afraid he'd beat me up if I didn't, and big surprise, I never saw that money again.

But I learned a principle there. Sometimes when you loan money to people, they avoid you if they can't pay you back. Because that kid, even though he was bigger than me, *avoided me* after that. I learned that money doesn't buy friendship. Help people if you can, but don't necessarily expect their friendship as a result. I didn't try to get the quarter back from him either, because he was bigger than me and I didn't know how he'd react. So we both stayed away from each other.

When I entered high school, I was fourteen and in the ninth grade. Perhaps because I was an only child, I was pretty quiet and introverted, not very outgoing except with my friends I gathered around me. I didn't like being an introvert. My father was a very quiet person, and my personality was more like his. I loved him but I looked at my mother, very much an extrovert and the belle of the ball, and I wanted to be more like that. I didn't like to be quiet. I was always loud and vocal in a one-on-one situation, even a small group of three. More people than that, and it was really hard for me to speak up.

So I remember very deliberately asking myself, "How do I overcome being an introvert? How do I become something that I'm not today?" It was such a valuable experience in my life trying to figure that out. I knew I had to get out of my comfort zone and the only way I saw to do that was in two different arenas: high school and church. I knew I had to force myself to be comfortable in front of larger groups of people and at least act like that person I wanted to be. Then figured I could become that person.

I had loved baseball growing up, so I could have played and believe I would have been successful. But I didn't think baseball would be the best in overcoming my weaknesses. So I literally jumped onto a stage and took high school drama. That turned out to be a great choice.

In my four years of high school, I took part in multiple plays. I didn't necessarily play the leading character; there was another boy in drama with me who I always thought would be a movie star. He had the look and skill for it; he had accents; he could play any role. He was fabulous, way better than I was. But I usually got the second biggest male part—a couple of them a year.

This accomplished its intended job: it forced me to get out of my comfort zone. I could look at the character I was playing—and it wasn't me. And if that character was an extrovert, which they all were, I could be an extrovert for the time I was playing that role. I portrayed characters who were outgoing and it began bringing me out of my shell. In my junior and senior years, I won the "Thespian of the Year" award. (It shocked me because I thought my friend would win.) That meant a lot to me. I had worked hard and tried to step outside myself to acquire skills I felt I needed. Looking back on it, I don't think I was the best overall actor, but I do know that I gave it everything I had.

Those awards and experiences gave me a lot of confidence going forward in my efforts to be comfortable in front of large groups. I was still quite an introvert in many ways, again to a large degree I think because I was an only child. Even at home during the week when my homework was done, I would sit and play board games if there was something preventing me from being with my friends, or them with me.

My church experiences as a youth were instrumental in helping me acquire leadership skills and kept me focused on my goal to be comfortable with groups of people. My bishop,

My high school graduation photo in 1963

or pastor, Lawrence Taylor, assigned me leadership positions among the youth. His attitude was, "You're in charge, you learn to lead." I loved him; he was a great leader. He knew how to give talks to the congregation without writing them down word-for-word, which I didn't know how to do. He taught our priesthood classes with stories, and he was very fluid and able to speak effortlessly. I would see him before he spoke in sacrament meetings just making his notes on a and index card and being able to get up and give fantastic talks. In a real way, he taught me how to be a leader among my peers. He was a great example to me and a man who had a significant impact on my young life.

Truthfully I wasn't a very good leader, not for a long time; I don't know how effective I was. But I knew I wanted to do well and *become* a good leader. Every Sunday one of my duties was to assign two or three young men to prepare and bless the bread and water for the sacrament to be passed through the congregation by other assigned priesthood holders. There was something I learned during that time period from one of the other boys. I'll call him Melvin. He was quite the ladies' man, which is fine, but in our church there is a standard of moral behavior to meet if you want to be worthy to participate in administering the sacred sacramental ordinance each Sabbath. One Sunday, Melvin came to me and said, "I'm not worthy to bless or pass the sacrament."

I didn't question it or judge him; it wasn't my role, but this taught me a valuable principle: we should always strive to be worthy in the eyes of God so we can continue to accomplish those good and noble things we seek in life. And we must be honest before God, first and foremost. It doesn't mean we go through life without stains or blemishes, because we're not perfect. But when we make mistakes, we need to learn how to overcome them, repent and turn back to God, because He's the author of all blessings in life. It took a lot of courage for Melvin to admit that he was not worthy that day. I'll never forget that.

During these years with these good people in my congregation, I was reluctantly introduced to not only the love of the written word, but found my own personal heroes. When I was about thirteen, there was a man in our church (and given that I rarely talked to anyone, I'm not sure how he picked me out) who brought me a book entitled *The First 2000 Years* by Cleon Skousen. He said he'd give it to me but wanted to make sure I would read it. I wasn't a reader but I agreed, and he badgered me every week. I said I'd do it and never did. I didn't *want* to read it, but I also didn't want to offend him. I finally thought I'd better do as I promised or he'd never stop asking me about it.

The book is about the first 2000 years of our mortal time line from Adam to Noah. I read the line of patriarchs with great interest—Adam, Seth, Cain, Abel, Methuselah, etc.— and they became my heroes. They were like celebrities to me. It put me on a track to read every church book I could get my hands on from then until I went on my mission. I loved it. That man must have been inspired to give me that book because I know it changed my life.

When I read it, I was reminded of my experience with

God five years before. Until then I'd kind of forgotten about how profound it was and hadn't given it much thought since. Now it returned in full force to my mind as I read about these great men and their relationships with God. It made me think of my own relationship with Him. And I thought that maybe, in my own way, I'm just as important as anyone else in life. You don't have to be an Adam or a Noah or an Eve to be loved and cared about by God. You just have to be you, the best *you* you can be. So it changed the direction of my life, where I probably would have been mediocre at best to where I felt I could accomplish whatever God wanted me to do.

> You just have to decide to be you, the best you "you" can be.

Every summer when I spent time with my cousin David, I'd relate those Bible stories to him. I learned later that David's mom used to sneak down the hallway and listen to me telling her son those stories. I used them on my mission, telling people about those great patriarchs and how they came to know God. I used their lives to inspire those I was teaching to try harder to become more like those great men. Those prophets changed my life and instilled a strong desire in me to live better.

And I didn't hate reading church books after that.

CHAPTER 6

I Never Want to See You Walking…

A S A TEEN, I ALWAYS WORKED. I wanted to make money. So I worked hard. My first job was at a Thrifti Mart in Bakersfield. I was a cart boy. On the weekends, I collected all the shopping carts from the parking lot and brought them back into the store. I even helped little old ladies out with their groceries.

When I was hired, bless that manager forever, he taught me the most valuable lesson with one sentence. "Ken, I never want to see you walking." Now I would push eight to ten carts at a time and I never walked that whole time I worked for him. I always looked around at the other guys and couldn't figure out why they were walking. Didn't he tell them the same thing? But I didn't criticize them. I just kept going as fast as I could, running if possible, except for when I carried groceries out for the little old ladies.

Many of these ladies wanted to tip me a quarter but I never took it because the manager had also told me not to accept tips. He taught me the concept of obedience to those for whom you work, to do your best, and to even go to the *extreme* to do your best. Never be a slacker. He taught me all about dependability, about the importance of being to work on time and doing what's expected.

One of the reasons I worked so hard in my teen years was to save money so I could serve a proselytizing mission for my church. These are self-financed missions and I wanted to be able to pay for it all myself. So at nineteen, I was a high school graduate and ready to go on my mission. I think I wanted to be a missionary more than anything in life at that time. Both of my parents had been missionaries. They initially met when they each served years earlier in the Northwestern States Mission. It covered Oregon, Washington, and the northern part of Idaho. I wanted to be a missionary because I was inspired by what they had accomplished. We look to those who blazed the trail before us, and I wanted to follow their example.

I suppose that's why it came as a shock when my parents told me they wanted me to attend one year of college before I went on a mission. I was so deflated! I wanted to go so badly. But I was obedient to my parents and the next Sunday the bishop called me in, obviously in cahoots with them. He also said he'd like me to go to college for a year before my mission. Looking back, I think the reason was because of my size and maturity level at the time. Just as it was to my benefit as a child to repeat that year in second grade, I think their theory was that another year before my mission would put me even with the rest of the pack. So I attended one year of college,

My parents with me at the Los Angeles LDS Temple in 1964,
prior to leaving for my mission for the Church of Jesus Christ of
Latter-day Saints to the Germany Frankfurt Mission for two-a-half years

begrudgingly, but forged ahead. It turned out to be a huge blessing in my life. I even went to summer school and had a year and a half of college under my belt before I went on my mission.

My eventual assignment was to the West Germany Mission, headquartered in Frankfurt, for two and a half years. Training is different now and missions these days are two years for young men (eighteen months for young women), but back then if it was a foreign assignment, an extra six months was tacked on to help the missionary learn the language. I was excited to go and one of my two very best friends was called to the same mission at the same time. We went together, which is very unusual.

This was my first experience outside the United States. We flew to Germany and were picked up by the mission president, his wife, and a couple of missionary leaders. They took us to the mission home, where they lived, and served us an authentic German meal. When we began the meal, they informed us that from that point forward, they would speak only German, no English. I should preface this by saying I was extremely poor at foreign languages. I had taken Latin and German and struggled with both classes. Linguistics just wasn't my area of expertise.

So there we were at our first meal in Germany and there was no English to be had. They'd told us a couple of German words for the food on the table and phrases applicable to the meal. But I didn't get very much to eat because I didn't know how to ask for anything. It was an interesting, even if annoying, approach—total immersion. We then had a couple days of training in the mission home after which I took the train to my first assignment, the German city of Worms. A long distance away.

Not speaking any German, I just hoped I would get on the right train because I had a transfer on the way down. It was a scary hour and a half journey. When I looked out the window I thought for sure I was going north instead of south for a while. I was worried I'd end up some place I wasn't supposed to be. Then what would I do? I was sitting in a train compartment halfway around the world from home and no one spoke English.

As we pulled into the train station, I saw the missionaries waiting for me and knew I had arrived at the right place. Latter-day Saint missionaries are paired in "companionships." My first companion, I'll bless his name forever, was Elder

Altman, a convert to the church and five years my senior. He was comforting to me—and much taller with a receding hairline. People sometimes mistook us for father and son. What a great missionary! He taught me how to do all the work and how to be effective. The first thing he told me when I met him was, "We don't go to movies." Going to a movie was the last thing on my mind; I thought it was a strange thing to say. What he was really telling me was, "We obey every rule."

He worked my fanny off! And every night he talked in his sleep. But in German. *Every night* I heard this German rattling from his mouth. Six weeks into it, I was starting to understand German, especially his, and I said, "Elder Altman, I'm going to understand every word you say in your sleep." Then the oddest thing happened—he never talked in his sleep again. My last two weeks with him, he just snored! And then I was transferred.

A year later I met his companion at a meeting and asked if Elder Altman still talked in his sleep in German. His companion said, "No, but he sure snores loud." I was convinced he'd learned not to talk in his sleep because of my comment. I should have kept my mouth shut. It would've been interesting to hear what he was talking about!

One of the best lessons I learned on my mission came from Elder Altman. He taught me how to be obedient to the rules. Rules that come from a worthy source are set up to teach us how to be successful. God doesn't punish us with

Follow the rules and you'll be more successful and happy.

commandments. He tells us, "Obey this and your life will be better!" I learned that's what mission rules are all about. Follow the rules and you'll be more successful and happy. I think about Elder Altman often. I learned so much from him.

I learned just the opposite from my next companion who wasn't a very hard worker. It turns out he and I were actually distant cousins, but he drove me insane and God left me with him for five and a half months. I thought, "I am *never* going to get away from this guy." He'd take us to movies, we'd go visit with people when we weren't supposed to, that sort of thing. He was "trunky," anxious to go home with a year still left on his mission.

I finally said, "Elder, if we don't stop breaking the rules, I'm going to write a letter to the mission president." I didn't like telling on someone, but I was the junior companion and was still learning. As the senior companion, he was in charge. I didn't like that, but I couldn't tell him what to do so he said, "Go ahead and write the letter!" I never did, but it was really peculiar to me that we stopped breaking the rules to the extent we were before.

I learned from him that disobedience means no success. You're not happy. I think God left me with him so long to teach me patience. That's one of my weakest attributes! If I decide I want to do something, it's gotta be done right now. In this case, I couldn't get anything done for five and a half months. Almost one-fifth of my mission I was with him. I didn't learn how to teach the lessons. I wasn't learning *anything* except my German was getting better, and I was able to read the Bible from the first page in Genesis to the last page in Revelation in German. I don't know how much I understood, but I did read it. And it helped me.

So even that turned out to be a learning experience for me. But by this time, I was so far behind. There were seven of us who had arrived in the mission at the same time. Two months shy of leaving this Elder, I was still a junior companion and all of the other six fellow missionaries who came out with me were already senior companions, including my best friend! They were doing so much better than me. I couldn't stand not being up leading the pack instead of trailing it. So it drove me even harder.

At eight months my next companion, Elder Raymond Johnson, said, "Elder Brailsford, when you leave me, you're going to be a senior companion." I don't think I really believed him because I was so discouraged. Not only was I *not* leading, I wasn't even up with the rest. This drove me crazy, not just because I wanted to be the leader, but because I'm short, I've always felt I had to prove that I'm as good as everyone else.

I was with Elder Johnson for three months and he taught me how to be a missionary like I'd never been taught before. I knew German by then; I could speak to anybody and say anything. I was coming out of my shell. And true to his word, at about eleven months into my mission, at my next transfer I became a senior companion. I went to a city called Darmstadt and was given a brand new missionary from the United States, Elder Dupree. He had to be 6' 3" or 6'4". He was so big and I was so short, if you know who Mutt and Jeff (Google them) are, that's who we looked like riding our bicycles down the road.

He was so willing to work and learn just as I'd been. I taught him how to be a missionary the way I wished I'd have been taught in terms of the whole process—the obedience, the routines, the teaching methods, the material. My first companion did teach me obedience and integrity, but he was mainly teaching me German. My second companion didn't teach me anything positive. So I wanted Elder Dupree, when he left me, to have the skills necessary to be a great missionary. And he was successful.

From there I became a District Leader where I was responsible for other missionaries in my district. I served in that capacity for the rest of my mission. Position and status truly didn't matter to me. What did matter was that I was doing what God wanted me to do. By the time returned home, I had been a District Leader longer than anyone in the whole mission. Most importantly, I'd learned to love the people with whom I worked, as well as the wonderful people of Germany.

I learned how to work hard on my mission. We had to record how many hours we worked, breaking it down into specifics, such as tracting (knocking on doors and sharing pamphlets), teaching lessons about religion to people, and testifying of the Savior. My companion and I were working about eighty hours a week. The only thing we did besides that was study and go to bed. That's all. In those days we were allowed to have three hours off—9:00 a.m. to noon each Monday. I only took one of those hours, just long enough to write a letter home. Then I was out the door at 10:00 a.m. working again.

The reason I worked more hours than anyone else was because I figured everyone else was better than me and I didn't want to get behind. I wanted to be more successful. I only remember one day, when I first became a senior companion, the District Leader said we were going to ride our bikes twenty miles up the road to look at an old castle up there and have a picnic.

When I was a District Leader, I was in Kassel, Germany. I borrowed that previous experience and used a castle there as incentive for the district. I took all eight of us, including my best friend who was in the same district, and we sat on a grassy hill overlooking that whole valley with the castle a couple hundred yards out and had our training on that beautiful spot. I told them, "If you work really hard this week and we have success, I'll give you an extra hour or so to tour that castle." Which we did! Other than the unfortunate time spent with my second companion, those were the only times in two and a half years that I took any time off to do anything. And I don't regret it to this day.

My first mission president was an interesting man, although rather distant and very serious. I wasn't around him very much so I didn't get to know him very well. But I could tell our personalities were quite different. I learned from him that with *my* personality, I couldn't lead the way he did.

About thirteen months into my mission, he returned home and we received a new mission president, Cecil Broadbent. I looked to President Broadbent as a mentor. I saw how dedicated he was and how hard he worked. I saw his spiritual strengths, his warmth, and love for others. He had dreams and visions and prophecies and every one of them came true. Right to the pinpoint of things. He was blessed with many of the spiritual gifts we read about in the scriptures. I admired that in him and I wanted to be like him.

I think as we grow up, our parents are our first mentors, then some of us get church leaders. My bishop was a mentor to me. Even many of my high school teachers had an influence on me for good. My second mission president was the same way. He taught me so much about the gospel and the scriptures. And he led me in all the ways I needed to be led. He taught me things I needed to know specifically to be a more effective leader.

At one point when I was a District Leader and had been for a while, we had twelve missionaries for whom I was responsible. Two of them were ladies, or what we call "sister missionaries." One of the sisters had known me about a year before and knew how introverted, shy, and quiet I'd been. Now all of a sudden, I was her District Leader! One of the other missionaries later told me she said, "When I heard Elder Brailsford was going to be my District Leader, I couldn't believe it. Now I see him and he's changed so much!"

I believed that if I learned from and followed wonderful mentors and strove to do my best, nothing could stop me from going right to the top! There was nothing special about me other than I had a great desire. I wanted to be successful. I wanted to be the best I could be. In terms of numbers, I had more success than any other missionary

> There was nothing special about me, other than I had a great desire.

in the whole mission while I was there, other than two of the sisters, and I could never duplicate what they did. They were so awesome. They set the pace for me.

I had nineteen companions over the course of thirty months. It was a complete crash course in how to get along with people 24/7 who come from different backgrounds and families. That's a lot of time to spend with a family member, let alone strangers! But the friendships I formed and the things I learned were invaluable. I grew on my mission in ways I would never have been able to otherwise.

I cherish the lessons I learned from my spiritual mentors as a young man. They forced me to reach beyond myself, beyond what I thought I was capable of. They reminded me to always look to God, to work hard and be diligent, and never give up. From my experiences in both high school and on my mission, I learned it is possible to change, to become someone better, to acquire skills and traits you may not have innately. It's never too late. We can and *should* always strive for improvement. We are never finished learning and growing.

And I still live my life by that one sentence: "Ken, I never want to see you walking."

CHAPTER 7

The Spirit of the Bayonet . . .

I WENT BACK HOME TO BAKERSFIELD after Germany and, in all that time I'd been gone, I thought I'd been spending my money from my mission fund. I found out that my parents had actually paid for the mission and my money was still sitting in the bank. They told me that the money was mine to start my life.

I was stunned and grateful. What a great thing my parents did for me in setting that example. Sometimes we need some help. And especially in my life, at that point, to have that money so I could get going and move forward was invaluable.

Shortly after my return home, a friend and I went to my former Thrifti Mart manager to ask about employment. He hired both of us on the spot, and in addition, I picked up work as a lab assistant in the college chemistry department and as a math and chemistry tutor. After the lab assistant job, I added a position as a security guard to my portfolio. The job was at my former high school where one of my main duties was to break up fights. I must have been effective because the kids listened to me. Except the girls. The advice I received upon taking the job was to stay out of the middle of a girl fight—and they were right. It was best to just pull them apart without getting in the middle of them. But with the boys, even being shorter, I could step between them and they'd stop fighting at once.

My next goal? I wanted to find a companion and begin my own family at that point. I had gone on my mission a little later than most young men, certainly longer than was typical, so I was a bit older and figured the time was right. I started to date a little bit. One day I was asked to teach a religion class for the young people in our area. There was a beautiful young lady in the class and I noticed her when I was teaching. I thought she was the prettiest girl I'd ever seen. When class was over, she visited with me and a couple of other guys, and I was thinking I should ask her out. Her name was Linda Hughes.

It took me a couple of weeks before I gave her a call. I said, "Linda, this is Ken Brailsford, and I'd sure like to take you on a date." I gave her the day and time and she said, "You know, I'm so sorry, I've got a date on that night. But call me again."

As I look back on that whole experience, if she hadn't told me to call again, I'm not sure I would have. I was a little insecure. Usually if I were rejected, I typically moved on. But I didn't this time, so I called her later and she went out with me. We dated for a while. Then on Valentine's Day, I proposed to her. We were married in July and have been together ever since, adding six wonderful children who blessed us with their spouses, grandchildren, even great grandchildren. We have all the blessings that come from finding the right companion and being bonded together, staying true to each other, and working through life's challenges.

That's what marriage brings—two different people from two different families, raised differently, who have to learn how to compromise. As the Bible says, you become "one flesh," and that takes time. The challenge for our young people today is they're sometimes not willing to pay the price and

Linda and me at our home in Orem about 1972

work through those challenges. There are so many divorces, and sadly, many of them could be worked through.

I was blessed to find the right companion. If I hadn't found Linda, I wouldn't have been able to accomplish any of the successes I've achieved. She's has always been loving and supportive, and that's exactly what I needed to go forward. Work has necessitated that I travel quite a bit through the years. I've been able to do that without worry because I always knew things were safe back home, that our kids were being cared for. I think God put her in my path and let me recognize her for who she was and marry her. She's very loving to everyone; she has no enemies. Her heart is full of charity. She'll give the shirt off her back if someone needs it. She loves our family above everything else and these are just a few of the things I love about her. She is also a woman with a deep, abiding love of God and is the perfect companion for me.

When we got married, I had two years of college under my belt from Bakersfield Junior College. We moved to Provo, Utah to go to Brigham Young University. Both of us worked. I had a job working forty hours a week washing dishes at the cafeteria on campus where I was paid a dollar an hour.

In all honesty, we couldn't have managed if we'd had to pay rent. My parents bought a home in Orem that they were going to move to upon retirement, so they let us live there rent free in the basement while I was going to school. That was a huge blessing. Before my father retired, they would come up from California and bring boxes of groceries to us. They were always supportive and always there for us.

I learned how hard it is to get a degree. I didn't take out

student loans and borrow money. I didn't have a Pell Grant like kids today. I didn't feel I was smart enough to apply for a scholarship, so I didn't. I just paid for it myself. One of my former missionary companions had his bachelor's degree in economics and I figured since I loved making money, why not be an economist?

So I got my degree in economics. I had no job and hadn't really even tried very hard to find one. I don't know what I was thinking at the time, but a job as an economist really wasn't to be. This was 1969, the Vietnam War was in full swing. I'd had a two and a half year deferral while I was a missionary, then a four year deferral for college. I assumed I might be drafted and figured I needed to go in the military and pay my dues. My mother told me once that she'd heard I could claim an exemption because I had small children, but I remember thinking that wasn't fair at all. Why should I be allowed to stay out of harm's way when another guy was obligated to go and risk his life?

As always with major decisions in my life, I prayed about it. The strong impression I received was that my time in the military would be similar to a mission. So I knew immediately I was supposed to go into the military and it was going to be a mission, although I didn't know what form it would take. I told Linda about it and we continued to pray for guidance. I realized I'd want to go into the Army and be an officer for a couple reasons. An officer gets paid more money and he doesn't have to wash dishes. I'd already done my share of dish washing.

I decided I'd enlist if I could go to Officer Candidate

School (OCS). I had no idea there was so much involved. I was interviewed by what I'll call a "tribunal" of three officers who had to approve me for OCS. After I received approval, I signed up for three years.

In June 1969, I found myself on my way to Fort Ord, California. The first six months were to be spent in basic training and advanced infantry training. The officers were nice to us initially—until we got to Fort Ord. Then everything changed. I had no idea what to expect in basic training. They were screaming and yelling four-letter words in our faces. I'd never experienced anything like it in my life. I was thinking *what have I gotten myself into?* One young man had the misfortune of wetting his pants, he was so unnerved. When the officers realized it, they pounced on him like a vulture on a carcass. We learned very quickly to avoid showing even the slightest weakness. The military had a way of taking the new recruits and treating them like meat in a grinder—putting it in whole and having it come out the other end all squashed and ground into one glob.

"What have I gotten myself into?"

The hard physical training for six to eight weeks was exhausting. I learned how to kill people with a bayonet and how to shoot a rifle. I knew that's what soldiers did but I didn't like it. It was a time of such intense conflict in Viet Nam that the Army needed to quickly turn average human beings into fighting machines. We were being trained to fight and would probably have to kill people. That was the assignment and they prepared us to do just that.

This is often a difficult mentality to reconcile for a lot of people. It certainly was that way for me. I look on the human soul as being so important, that we are all children of God, regardless of race, color, or where we live in the world. I believe we are all brothers and sisters of one enormous family, so being trained to kill with a bayonet or a rifle and bullet was incredibly hard. It made me think a lot.

During drills we would thrust the bayonet into a "dummy," kind of like a scarecrow. Then the instructors would shout, "What's the spirit of a bayonet?" and we'd have to yell back, "To kill, to kill, to kill!" They drilled it *over and over* into our heads, so if we ever faced a combatant, we wouldn't hesitate to thrust that bayonet or shoot the rifle and kill the enemy.

This training was routine until we heard a news team was coming to film basic training. The drill instructor said, "If they come today or tomorrow during training, we won't say, 'What's the spirit of the bayonet?' And you won't say anything." They didn't want the news media to know about this, which I thought was a bunch of bologna. They were training us to be killers and yet didn't want the rest of America to see it. The film crew never did end up coming to our training session, which was probably just as well.

After basic I went into advanced infantry training. Here the interesting thing was the diversity of people. There were sixty of us who started out together; some would wash out or have to repeat. Some didn't pass the physical test. These were challenges in themselves anyway. But we had one individual in there who hated our instructor so much he said, "If I ever get a chance, I'm going to kill him." And he really meant it.

The monkey bars at Ft. Belvoir in 1970—my last PT test in OCS

I steered clear of that guy from then on. That was an attitude too far from my realm of comprehension.

There were times during my training where I felt almost

tortured. One time at OCS, we went on a Saturday run in formation with our rifles, backpacks and combat boots. We had canteens of water and were told to make sure they were full. It was summer and we were sweaty and exhausted, running between trees, couldn't stay in formation. The tactical officer, Lieutenant Bundy, stopped us and said, "You guys didn't stay in formation. You're going to fill your mouths up with one mouthful of water. Do not swallow it. Then you're going to run up that hill and when you get to the top of it, you had better spit the water out or you will be in trouble."

Some of the guys had hesitated to put water in their canteens, thinking it wasn't going to be that long of a run and didn't want to carry that extra weight. But I had water in mine so I got a mouthful and we started to run in formation up that hill. Now if you have to run up a hill, most of the time you run with your mouth open, gasping for air, trying to breathe. You can't do that with a mouthful of water. We had to breathe through our noses unless we wanted to swallow the water. But I knew what was coming if I swallowed mine, so I decided I wouldn't swallow even if I dropped over dead.

I ran up, breathing so heavily and hard through my nose that I had snot all over my face, lungs burning. It was horrible. As each soldier got to the top, the tactical officer grabbed him by the shirt and said, "Spit the water out." Those who had the water to spit out went over on one side. Those who didn't, went on the other side. About a third of the guys didn't have any water to spit out. Whether they'd started with any or not, I don't know, but that was the end of the course for the day. The two-thirds of us who had water in our mouths got to go back to the billets (barracks for officers) and take the rest of the day off. The third who didn't have the water had to go down with the tactical officer and go through a couple hours of heavy punishment exercises referred to as "grass drilling," which is not something you ever want to experience in the military. It went something like this: "Drop and give me five! On your feet! Drop and give me ten! On your feet! Drop and assume dying cockroach position!" And "dying cockroach position" meant lying on your back, arms and legs extended straight into the air, and held there for usually ten to fifteen minutes or longer, depending on the tactical officer's whim.

This was the kind of training that made me re-evaluate everything. It was a strange form of refiner's fire, one that often had me conflicted and uncomfortable, but I'm grateful for it. It taught me that many things in life aren't always comfortable. Sometimes we have to do things we don't want to do. But they can give us the opportunity to grow.

CHAPTER 8

A Second Mission . . .

A
FTER FINISHING MY TRAINING at Fort Ord, there were
six of us with orders to go to Office Candidate School.
One of those six had graduated in engineering but received
orders for infantry, while I received orders for engineering.
When you enlisted in OCS, you got to choose either artillery,
infantry, or engineering. I knew I didn't want to be an artillery
or engineering officer. That left the infantry, so I signed up for
that. I didn't realize that there was small print in the contract.
I never could understand the rationale of the Army regarding
those assignments. It seems that I took that engineer's place
and he took mine.

So Linda and I headed for Ft. Belvoir, Virginia with about
a month to get there and find an apartment for her to live in
for the next six months. Our son, Kenny, stayed with his
grandmother Hughes. She flew with him to Virginia to meet
us when we got there and were settled.

I've seen God's intervention in my life multiple times and

on this road trip to Virginia I was reminded of His constant presence. We were driving through Oklahoma. I was anxious to get across the country and was driving about ten miles an hour over the speed limit. It was raining cats and dogs on the freeway, just a dense, thick rain.

Luckily there were no other cars within about a hundred to two hundred feet when I hit a slick spot. My car started to spin. I had no way of controlling it going at that speed. It continued moving in the same direction, rotating as if on a pivot. Hydroplaning, the car completed a full 360 degrees before it stopped spinning. It kept going down the freeway. If it had stopped at anything less than 360 degrees, we'd have been off the freeway and probably died in the wreckage. It was one of those moments when Linda and I were aware we'd been spared. As we continued driving, Linda said a prayer and thanked God for preserving our lives.

We made it in one piece to Virginia, found a place to live in a basement, and got our little family set up with about a week to spare before beginning OCS. The purpose of OCS was to teach us how to be officers, how to give commands, how to lead people by putting ourselves in the front. If you're a platoon officer, you're in the front. You're leading. And you're the most likely to be killed first in combat. While training, I heard that during WWII, platoon leaders (2nd and 1st lieutenants) lived on average seven days in combat, while sergeants had a life expectancy of one month in combat.

I knew OCS was going to be an interesting ride when I first arrived. I had to find the tactical shack (where the tactical officers had their offices) and no one had told us where it was. I thought everyone would be nice, especially if they were officers. So I went running up to one of four officers standing together (it was not permitted to ever walk as a new officer candidate) and in the required form of address said, "Sir, Candidate Brailsford. Can you tell me where the tactical shack is?"

And he looked at me, put his face right in mine and said, "Do I look like a tour guide? Get the hell outta here!"

I had to take off. I finally found it on my own. But after that I was always afraid to ask questions of any officer because they treated you so poorly. Those were experiences that at the time made me think I must be worthless, but then I came out the other end and I'd learned how to treat people. We were treated so poorly as candidates, I learned to do the exact opposite when it came to real life outside the military. It made me think about life, about the value of other people.

We learned about engineering, how to build pontoon bridges over a river, all those physical things that were necessary to know before heading overseas. I met some wonderful people who I could have been best friends with forever; others I was happy to work with, but outside of that training we didn't necessarily want each other as friends.

Perhaps one of the most valuable tools I gained from this experience that has carried over to my business life quite profoundly is the skill for making command decisions. What are those exactly? They're decisions where you take all of the intelligence or information you have before you to make an instant decision. The importance of learning this skill in the military setting was crucial. Some people, after gathering all

The worst possible decision is not making one at all.

the information, can't decide what to do, and the situation goes on and on and is never resolved. In combat, you can't do that. You and your men could be dead.

The best decision is a quick, correct one; the next best decision is a bad one; and the worst possible decision is not making one at all.

I still make decisions that way today because I know if I make a bad decision, unless it's a life and death one, I can back up and correct it. If I sit there not making decisions, my business could be destroyed from inaction. I've stuck with the philosophy of the importance of the command decision. It doesn't mean I'm always right, but generally I've been able to back out and correct the bad ones.

After you make a decision, you put it into action. You have to do that in life. Make decisions and be willing to stick with them unless you realize quickly it's a bad decision and you can course correct right there on the spot. From that point, go forward and make another command decision.

In OCS, we were graded over a six month period. I got to go home and be with my wife and son, Kenny, three nights during that whole six months. The tactical officers were determined to make us buckle under pressure by looking for our weaknesses. They try to wash you out and get rid of you. In my case, they focused on demerits. We'd have our weekly inspection and when the tactical officer came to me, looking at my uniform, he always gave me "golf suit" demerits. A golf suit is where the shirt doesn't match the pants; one's faded out worse than the other. After you've been there for a while, they're *all* faded out, no two pieces match exactly. And being color blind (did I mention that?), I probably had a harder time than anyone. After I received a demerit every week, I'd look at the soldier next to me, his "golf suit" worse than mine, but he didn't get a demerit!

So I would always get demerits. Usually on Saturdays, when most of the other guys went home to be with their wives, I had to march to cadence in a twenty-foot square with my rifle for about four hours. That was how they tried to put pressure on me, and it was especially stressful for Linda. But I learned how to obey and do things I didn't like to do. That was the whole purpose.

We were ranked, in their mind, from the best to the worst with no two people being equal. They would give us a score that would count as two-thirds of our points. Then we would be rated by our peers as well, and that score counted as the final third. When I first got there, my leadership style was at odds with the military method. I had learned my skills through church and missionary service which meant I led with love, kindness and a quiet voice. With that as my approach in OCS, I was a disaster.

The first rating came out the second month I was there. I was in the bottom third of sixty of us. I didn't like that and realized fairly quickly that my personal style wasn't going to cut it. I didn't want to wash out so something had to change. I had to become mean like the rest of them.

So from that point forward when I had leadership positions within the platoon, I changed my approach. I adopted the harsh, unyielding, and unforgiving attitude that came with the environment. The next time we were rated, I was in the top third—the exact reverse of where I'd been. I learned in certain situations you've got to be tough, quick, and agile, or you simply will not survive. It depends on your circumstances, of course, and the setting in which you find yourself. This particular training was preparing us to lead others into battle in life and death situations. You'd better move fast and insist on strict obedience from your men because lives depended on it.

This wasn't an easy transition for me. But there was more at stake than just my own personal ambition to do well. This was my job and potentially a career that would support my family if I were to eventually choose that route. I couldn't afford to fail and yet that brutal atmosphere was so foreign to anything I'd known that it almost washed me out. My scores on tests were always good, but my peer reviews were terrible. I had to change my whole outlook so I would survive and rise to the top, which I did. I wasn't #1, but I certainly wasn't #40 by the time we graduated. At the end of this course, there were only forty of us remaining of the original sixty.

You learn to do what you have to do to become successful. The interesting part was that the tactical officers who gave us such grief for that training period were really only six months ahead of where we were. It was almost a hate thing with them on our part because every time we saw them, they brought pain, usually literally. You come as close to hate as you can and still try to love God.

The training required that the first two words out of my mouth were always "Candidate Brailsford." This was always the preface to anything I would say to the officers. I remember reaching the same rank as the tactical officers at the end of the training. As I passed by them with my gold bars on my shoulders, just like theirs, Lieutenant Peterson (the senior tactical officer at the time) put his hand out and shaking mine. He didn't say, "Congratulations, Candidate Brailsford," Instead he said, "Congratulations, Ken."

It was such a weird change I didn't know if I wanted to slug him or thank him. The change in address, demeanor, *everything* was instantaneous because now I was his peer. We were both 2nd Lieutenants.

> I didn't know if I wanted to slug him or thank him.

Ironically enough, the way we were taught to lead in OCS wasn't effective even in a war zone. In combat, if you lead like they were teaching us, your own men would kill you in Vietnam. A study followed five tactical officers who went to Vietnam after their OCS assignment and, out of the five, three of them were killed by their own men; one was killed by the enemy; and only one came home alive.

Several of us from OCS were sent to North Carolina after six weeks of training in military intelligence. At that time, we expected to be there for three months. Then all of the new 2nd Lieutenants, after those three months in their duty, were supposed to be shipped to Vietnam. That was our full expectation, but it never happened. The Army started to reduce the number of soldiers in Vietnam about that time, and no one that went to Fort Bragg in our group ever got orders for Vietnam.

My first assignment was to the intelligence battalion at

Ft. Bragg—the Continental Army Command Intelligence Center (CONTIC). In my time spent as an officer, I didn't lead the way I'd been taught. I led by allowing my people to know I cared about them. I wanted them to be successful. I didn't care about unpolished shoes or long hair, within reason, but I did care about their job performance.

So much of the military mentality continued to be frustrating to me. We had frequent visits from our battalion commander, a full bird colonel, and every time he walked though my department he'd come back and say to me, "Lieutenant Brailsford, DeVoe needs a haircut. Make him get one."

I'd say, "Yes sir," and go back to DeVoe and tell him the Colonel wanted him to get a haircut. He'd acquiesce and do it. I never understood why the company commander didn't stay on top of that—they did an inspection at 6 a.m. every day for that purpose.

In my department I had an NCO (non-commissioned officer) who worked for me (a great guy, Sergeant Irwin), a civilian (Mr. Lockamie), and twelve enlisted men. We worked with a big behemoth of a machine that could read classified (secret) documents. It had been coded to pick out certain things that we printed and gave to the analysts whose job it was to analyze military strategies and abilities for certain armies in various countries throughout the world. It was a great job and I loved the people I worked with.

There were times during that first year of military service that I reconsidered, thinking I'd made a mistake. In that controlled environment, I couldn't do much missionary work. I knew what I'd felt initially, the impression I'd had that this would be another mission, but so far I hadn't seen that happening. I did became close with a couple of officer candidates and, in that way, I was a missionary for them, but I'd still really been waiting for that promised missionary experience.

While at Ft. Bragg, I worked during the day and at night I could do missionary work. This was where I started to see that original inspiration come to fruition. I could go meet people and talk to them about the church and Christ. I did this two or three nights a week and it became a great experience for me, My second mission was finally happening for me as I'd hoped before I joined the Army.

I enjoyed this time, especially after the rigors of training. What I had was a real job. I went home at night and was never bothered unless I was the night duty officer. But because I was an officer, I always had an NCO with me. Officers got to sleep while the NCO had to stay awake. That's the way the Army ran. But I felt guilty, so I didn't sleep as much as some of the others probably did. It wasn't that comfortable anyway; you slept in your duty fatigues on top of a cleared off desk.

The civilian who worked with me, Mr. Lockamie, was the man who inadvertently taught me that betting is a fool's game unless you have concrete knowledge to support your bet. He made a habit of walking around the office betting anyone a Coke if they knew the answer to such and such a question. What nobody realized was that he'd researched the answers ahead of time, so he never lost a bet. I don't think he ever had to buy his own Coke. I lost a bet to him once and that was enough.

Mr. Lockamie was paid a lot of money to be there. He was the tech guy that kept the big machine from breaking; he kept it running. He certainly made more than I did as an officer and his company was paid just to have him there.

He and I strategized one time. *How could we save the Army money?* We had a lot of payroll; we paid from $20,000 to $30,000 for paper every year; we had this big machine with all of its maintenance; Mr. Lockamie's wages; and his company's compensation. So we devised a strategy.

I took that information and went in to see my boss who was a Lieutenant Colonel. As I stood at attention in front of his desk, I said, "Mr. Lockamie and I have come up with some ways to save the Army a lot of money." He asked what it was and I went through what we'd come up with, piece by piece. At the end I said, "We can do this, make the change, not interrupt service, or any challenges to anything being done here for a $5,000 investment." The investment was a specialized camera that we needed, just one for the job. This plan eliminated the big behemoth of a machine, my position, the civilian position, and nine enlisted men, leaving only three enlisted men and an NCO to run the department.

And he immediately said, "Nope. We're not going to do that." I said, "Sir, why not?"

He said "Because this is our showplace. This is where we bring all our generals when they come around."

That was true. I'd given tours at least once every six to eight weeks, including one to the highest ranking four-star General in the continental U.S. at the time, and I was thinking, *Okay, but this will save a lot of money! Millions of dollars.* My assumption upon entering that office had been that he would send me out to put the plan on paper so he could take it up the line to the full bird Colonel, who was the battalion commander. In the Army you can't go around people to their superiors or you'd be in serious trouble. There wasn't anything more I could do, so the proposal died before it ever took off.

I should have known this plan of ours wasn't going to work because there had been a big newspaper article not too long before our presentation that reported the Army at Ft. Bragg was saving millions of dollars a year by terminating 150 civilian employees. If you read the article and didn't know anything you'd think, "That's great! They're saving money! What a wonderful bunch of people trying to save the taxpayers' money!" Well, what they had actually done was taken those people and simply reassigned them to a different department. If you didn't know that part of the story it looked like they'd saved millions a year. In reality they saved nothing. I just couldn't cope with that thought process.

In the end, my mind was made up. I realized the military wasn't for me. I knew I couldn't work with people who don't think like business people. I knew that for myself, I had to do something different. I can't work with people who won't do the most efficient thing and who can't do the right thing.

I look back on my military experience, even the hard times, and I learned so much. I even had spiritual experiences in the Army that became highlights of my life to that point. The military taught me not only leadership skills as an officer, but also simply how to deal with people, superior officers as well as enlisted men. I learned how to better accomplish the goals assigned to me. My strength, both physical and mental, was tested to the maximum and I learned that I was tougher than I thought.

2nd Lieutenant, U. S. Army, Kenneth Earl Brailsford,
new graduate of OCS 1970

CHAPTER 9

I Think I Have Something You'd Be Interested In . . .

M Y INTEREST IN BUSINESS extends back to childhood. I don't remember a time when I haven't found it fascinating. My family's only foray into the business world, however, was a business venture that became a nightmare for my parents.

My father was still going to school for his PhD and the business that caught his eye was related to chemistry. He and a couple friends purchased a small skin care company. My parents were always frugal, never spent money foolishly or wasted it. My dad's investment was $5,000—everything he and my mother had saved.

I remember being so excited and proud, going with my dad one time to the factory. It was just a small business and it must have been a Saturday because nobody was working. I looked at those stainless steel vats, the production line, and I was completely enthralled. My father was also excited and

I wonder if this was one of those unconscious signals that pointed me toward business later.

Sadly, his happiness was short-lived. The very man that my father and the others had bought the business from—and trusted—was cheating them. They ran out of money and went broke. The former owner was completely dishonest and was supposedly a religious person, which made the sting all the more painful.

It was a very sad situation and my parents could have been very bitter. They could have sued him but yet they didn't. They forgave him and went on with their lives, having lost that investment. I learned a lot from them because of that. First of all, I don't like law suits. I don't like suing and I certainly don't like to be sued. I learned to be forgiving like my parents were. It doesn't take me anything to forgive people, even if they've seriously hurt me. Holding onto that anger is unfair to them and brings only negativity and bad feelings into my life.

The experience with that failed business eventually took a backseat in my memories as my young life progressed, but that feeling of excitement and anticipation of a new venture lingered until the time was right.

When I lived in California as a teen with my parents, every summer we'd go back to Utah and visit family. When I was thirteen, my mother had a health issue. (And remember, in those days, nobody knew anything about herbs unless you'd been a hippie.) So that particular summer, my mother told a friend in Salt Lake about her health issue. Her friend said that there was an herb growing by the side of the road in southern Utah called chaparral. She described the plant and recommended that we stop when we found it. She said if my mother would strip the leaves off the plant, put them in a sack, take them home, steep them into a tea, and drink a cup every day, she'd never have that health issue again.

My mother took chances and believed in people, and she was willing to try anything. I remember that summer drawing to a close, school was almost ready to start, so we drove back home, stopping on the way when we found the chaparral plant by the side of the road. We got out of the car. I had to do most of the leaf-picking while my parents watched. We had this big paper sack from the grocery store, and I was out there in the heat, picking and stripping those leaves off the plant and putting them into the paper sack. I filled it full, not realizing that before long I'd regret that. My first clue that I was in for something crazy should have been when I noticed that my hands had turned solid green. I was pretty horrified, and I don't remember how I got them clean—we were out in the desert on the highway in the days before hand sanitizer and wet wipes.

When we got home, my mother was anxious to start making that tea. So she sat in the kitchen, boiled a pot of water, put a handful of leaves into it, and let it sit there a couple of minutes. As I watched, before long I saw green mist coming up out of the pot. The next thing I knew, we were sitting there enveloped in a cloud of green. It was awful looking and it smelled worse!

I watched, wondering what was coming next, and my mother proceeded to pour three cups of this green tea. One for me, one for her, and one for Dad. About that time, my dad walked into the kitchen, saw the green mist, smelled the disgusting stench, and promptly turned around making a beeline out. He never, ever drank that stuff. He wouldn't get near it. So my mother turned to me and I thought, *Oh no. It's my turn.* I was too young and I knew my mother. I was not going to be able to turn around and walk out.

She said, "Here's your cup."

I thought, *Why do I have to be first with this thing?* I went over by the kitchen sink, reasoning if it tasted as bad as it smelled and looked, I didn't know if it'd stay down. I'd heard something about plugging your nose to choke down something that tasted bad, so I was hopeful I could get it down in two or three big gulps.

So I did it. Stood over the sink, held my nose, and down went that cup of tea—three swallows. I hung over the sink as my stomach started to rumble. I thought, *Oh no, it's coming out!* Pretty soon, though, my stomach settled down and I realized I'd survived.

I looked over at Mom. She had a very sensitive stomach. She gagged and almost threw up, had a horrible experience with it, but it was great fun for me to watch since she'd made me be the guinea pig. But she did keep the tea down.

I figured we'd tried it and would never have to drink it again since the previous day's experience had been so bad. School started the next day and I came home in the afternoon to see that lousy cup of tea waiting for me, ready to go. I had to drink it every day along with my mom. My dad never did, so the leaves lasted a long time. I completely regretted picking so much of that stuff!

Here's the interesting thing, though. My mother, to the day she died, never had that health issue again. And another thing I noticed was that as a young teen I was starting to get acne, which is such a big social thing to a teenager, but when I drank that nasty brew, my acne cleared up. When I stopped drinking the tea, the acne started coming back again. But every summer after that when we would drive by that area in southern Utah where the chaparral grew in abundance, we never stopped. It tasted so nasty that there was no mention ever again about getting more. My mother's health was better and I wasn't concerned enough about the acne to choke down any more of that tea.

Here, though, is where I see the invisible hand of God at work. Why would my mother's friend have mentioned this herb growing on the side of the road in the desert? This is the beginning of that hand guiding me throughout my life. Everything that followed either paved the way or prepared me for the path my life took after my time in the military.

Directly following my release from the Army, we moved back to Utah to be near family and had the incident I related earlier with the cayenne pepper capsules and Gene's ulcers. That was the beginning of Nature's Sunshine Products. We were clueless about how to sell the product. We learned as we stumbled along. We had our product and I had to be the salesman. I don't know how I got elected, but Gene went with me, driving his little Volkswagen Bug. We put those thirty bottles in the back seat that we'd produced by hand and tried to figure out where we should go first.

There was a little place down the street called Cottage Health Food Store, so we decided to try that first. It was a little narrow store with some racks on the side of one wall and the counter on the other side. I had never sold anything like this in my life so I decided to take just one bottle in. Gene entered behind me (always behind me!) and a sweet little lady, Emma Chittock, the store proprietor, approached us.

I said, "I have a product I think you'd be interested in," and handed her the bottle. She took it in her hand. What I didn't know then was that that's half the sale. When talking to customers, get the product in their hand. Don't stand there and explain it. Luckily, I didn't know what to say, so I kept my trap shut. If you say something first when you hand it to them, you'll lose the sale.

Pretty soon she turned to me and said, "So, how much is this?"

How much is it? I hadn't even thought about that. I didn't even factor the hours of labor into this thing, but I figured the raw cost at about a dollar a bottle. I thought quickly, not wanting to lose the sale, and said, "How about $1.15 a bottle." Fifteen cents profit? That wouldn't even come close to compensating for labor—it would have been way lower than minimum wage!

She said, "Okay, I'll write you a check for $6.90. I'd like six of them." Gene went out to the car and got five more. She put them on the shelf on this big wall of products. Our first sale! We were so elated! The we tried to decide where to go next.

We drove down to the grocery store since we weren't aware of other health food stores nearby. This had to have been the craziest grocery store I'd ever been in. The manager's office wasn't even an office. We had to go up rickety stairs to the second level only to find plywood laying on the beams up above all the freezers. And there was nothing up there but his desk in the back corner. He was sitting there with his back to us and as we were walking across those plywood sheets, I held my one bottle thinking, *Okay, it worked last time. I'm going to use the same approach.*

He finally looked over his shoulder to see us and I approached with Gene, of course, behind me. I gave the manager the bottle and figured he'd tell me how many bottles he wanted after asking the price, just like Emma Chittock had. But this manager looked at me and said, "Well, why would I want this product?"

I thought, *Hey, that wasn't in the script!* So I figured the best thing to do would be to relate Gene's story. He then said, "Okay, I'll take 144 bottles."

This was the only time in my life I've ever talked someone down from a sale. I said, "Would you settle on twenty-four?" and he said he would. Gene went to the car to get the remaining bottles and the manager wrote a check at $1.15 a bottle.

We went downstairs with him and he put the bottles by the cash registers. I thought it was pretty good placement, except he set them on shelves next to the candy. And that made no sense to me—*why would you put this next to candy?* But I didn't say anything to him about it.

So we left with the check and went back to the house to tell everyone. We were all thrilled! We'd sold all thirty bottles! It was time to get back to work. Then it dawned on me that I hadn't calculated any labor into the cost. We were losing our shirts!

So I changed the price to $1.60 a bottle. We went back to Emma's store a week later to see how the product was selling. We'd sold one bottle in a week and I thought that wasn't bad. And it wasn't long before she reordered. Soon after, she reordered every week.

We went back to the grocery store time after time and nobody bought any of the cayenne pepper there for months. It never sold at that location. Pretty soon the dust started to gather on the bottles and I told Gene we'd better not go back there anymore—the manager might eventually ask us for a refund. We never did go back after that. Emma kept buying, though, and now we needed to decide what to do for a second product as we expanded our sales territory. Health food stores were great for our product. I was a salesman for a long time as we expanded the territory and I never had one "no" at any health food store I went to.

Not surprisingly, the next product was chaparral. Do you see the hand of God in this? He planted that knowledge of the health benefits of this plant over ten years before, when I was a young teen, so that when I came to this point, that experience became Nature's Sunshine's next product.

In an odd sort of history-repeating-itself way, we went to southern Utah to strip leaves off those bushes, just as I'd done as a kid. And this time there were a lot of them. We had the whole backseat stuffed full of gunny sacks of chaparral leaves. We realized we couldn't cram entire leaves into a capsule and knew we'd have to turn it into a powder. So we put our heads together when we returned home and decided Gene's little wheat grinder would do the job nicely. Gene was a school teacher during the day and every night, when he came home, he'd stuff those leaves in the top of the grinder and crank the handle, grinding them into powder. It was then I decided I had the better end of the deal with the sales job and told Gene to keep grinding.

We expanded that little line and it grew. Two years later, we turned it into an multi-level marketing (MLM) company. It was amazing. In those days, the MLM industry was in its infancy. There were a few companies—Amway, Shaklee—I believe about six total in the world, and then there was us, Nature's Sunshine Products. The first distributor I went out and found myself was Jack Ritchason. My mother knew Jack—they went to the same church. After we started Nature's Sunshine I remember her saying we needed to come to Bakersfield and recruit him. He was with Shaklee at the time and her impression was that he would do a great job for our company.

I had a long conversation with Jack and his wife, Verlyn, talking for several hours about Nature's Sunshine. Then he told me, "Ken, I'm making a lot of money with Shaklee. If I join your company and they threaten to cut me off because of it, you know who I'll have to go with." And we both knew he meant Shaklee. But it wasn't long before he was making more with us and pretty soon he didn't do Shaklee anymore.

The conversation that night was memorable and pivotal for me and the business. It was also funny because when his bedtime rolled around at ten o'clock that night, he just stood up and said, "Well, I'm going to bed. You guys can stay here and talk all night if you want." So Verlyn and I talked for another couple of hours. She was even more convinced than Jack that they should join our company.

We had another top leader, Delloy Abplanalp, who really helped us gain momentum in MLM. The first time he came to our office/warehouse, he purchased $1000 worth of our products, the largest order we had ever received. It was huge! We filled his trunk and backseat up with our products and he drove back to his home in California. I looked at Dick, one of my partners, and said, "We'll never see Delloy again." Three nights later, about one in the morning, Delloy called me to say, "I need another thousand dollars' worth of product. Would you send it first thing in the morning?" I was flabbergasted and in shock. I asked him how he had done it.

The first meetings he held were in a chicken coop.

Delloy held his first meeting in a chicken coop that he'd cleaned up in his backyard and turned into a meeting room. Every night for weeks he would call me up, duplicating his $1000 order. Then every morning we'd get the product packaged up, put it on a Greyhound bus, and the oder would arrive in California the next day.

We had a meeting for Delloy in California. Jack Ritchason attended it, having heard about Delloy's success, He was especially impressed to see so many people at the meeting. Afterwards, Jack found me and said, "I want you to know I'm going to be your biggest and best distributor." So Jack went to work covering the whole country. He had a motor home he drove all over, recruited, built his business—he really became the best.

For a while I'd say to Delloy, "You know, Jack's starting to make more money than you." Then I'd call Jack and say, "Delloy's starting to make more money than you." They'd both work harder and recruit more and hold more meetings. Then I'd call them both and go back and forth like that over time until all of a sudden Jack left Delloy in his rear-view mirror and got so far ahead I couldn't use that tactic anymore.

Jack is the one who taught me so many things about this MLM industry. Because there were so few of us around at the time, I relied heavily on Jack's influence and suggestions; he taught me as we went along. He never asked for anything; he wasn't greedy; he didn't expect more than anybody else; he didn't expect a special deal; he didn't expect me to give people to him if they were "orphans"; he just worked. He worked hard and he helped people. He was always at the top of our company.

Over the years as I worked with him, we became very good friends. I always trusted what he told me. There was no hidden agenda with Jack. His friendship and his business acumen were invaluable to me, and I was always grateful to have had that association with him.

The company was growing and becoming bigger than our health food store side of the business. I decided to drop that portion of our business as I was getting complaints from our distributors. That was one of my bad decisions in life. If I had kept that side of the business, I could have controlled the competition. When you leave a void as I did, someone steps in and you've created your own competition. They aren't as accommodating to you as you would be to yourself. I should have told the distributors that it was all right to keep the stores and I would make sure it wouldn't hurt them in the field. But I had followed what they said. I learned that just because people tell you things, you have to learn it's not always the right thing to do. They don't have all of the information. It may appear to be the right thing to do on the surface, but there are always unintended consequences, and there were certainly unintended consequences for this decision.

When the business started, it was all about having a job and a business and creating an income. That was the purpose behind what we were doing and the emphasis, in my mind, wasn't on health benefits, other than as the main thrust behind the sale. But a couple years after we got started, we began having small meetings with a few distributors. One particular gathering stands out in my mind as the pivotal point on which everything shifted for me.

We were in a little room with a podium up front, having a testimony meeting. People came up and shared their experiences with the products. One little lady, I remember as if it were yesterday, said, "You know, I had cancer. The doctors did everything they could do for me and sent me home to die. I took your products and I don't have cancer anymore."

I don't know if she was completely correct or not, but it was a monumental moment for me. My "why," my driving purpose, changed from the notion that I was merely creating an income to provide for my family. My mantra instead became *I'm helping people change their lives for the better.*

That kind of shift in my "why" was huge. So again, placed right in my path was one little lady who shared her experiences, and it changed my entire frame of thought as it concerned this business. If it would have been anyone else in that meeting, my "why" wouldn't have shifted and the end result wouldn't have been the same. Again, I clearly saw the invisible hand of God.

I like to learn new things and experiment, and I see threads of my young life in this process. Because we moved so much when I was a child, it was as though I was always looking forward to the new adventure with a sense of anticipation. I like to create businesses. I like to invest in and save businesses in trouble. And over the years, there have been times I've thought, *Maybe it's time for me to exit and do something else.* It really is uncanny but it's so real to me that it's just the invisible hand of God. As I tried to walk out of Nature's Sunshine, more than once, it was almost like He put a hand on my shoulder and pulled me back. It's symbolic, of course, but I couldn't exit. I wanted to, but I couldn't.

In the meantime, this was the '70s, and people would ask what I did for a living. I would respond that I sold herbs. "Oh, you mean spices?" was the inevitable response. Nobody knew anything about traditional herbs. There was a great disconnect between education and telling people how to use these products.

Because of that disconnect, we started an educational company that published herbal books and a magazine. This was the first herbal magazine in the marketplace at that time. If it was still being published today, it would literally be selling millions of copies. It was there before *Men's Health* or any of the health magazines so prevalent now, other than *Prevention Magazine*. I was running Nature's Sunshine and owned 100% of this educational publishing company but I had quite a lot on my plate. So I hired a man in New York who was an "expert" to run the publishing end. But every month when I got my financial statement, I realized that the "expert" was losing money—big time.

Finally in November 1979, I received the last financial statement from this guy that showed a $40,000 loss in one month. The losses were almost doubling monthly. I figured the next month the loss would be $80,000 and I knew he was going to bankrupt me. I didn't have that kind of money to lose.

He was in New York City on a business trip when I called him and fired him over the phone. In one day I had to literally leave Nature's Sunshine and step over in my role with the hemorrhaging publishing company before it destroyed me financially. That time there was no invisible hand pulling me back. It was time for me to make that exit.

Publishing is a very hard business, but I turned the losses around from $40,000 in November to less than $10,000 the next month, and our losses kept decreasing every month after that. It was a huge challenge. It seemed we needed a large circulation to get more advertising, and we needed more advertising to get a larger circulation. It was like a dog chasing its own tail. When the time was right, I sold it because it was time to move on.

By 1985, I'd been out of the nutritional/MLM business for a couple years when Jack Ritchason contacted me and said he wanted me to start another MLM. I said, "Why would I want to do that, Jack?"

He said, "Because Nature's Sunshine is making some business decisions that I don't agree with and I want to have a place for the distributors to go when they aren't happy about it."

I told Jack I'd see what I could do. I mentioned this to Dave, another friend of mine. Dave told me about a little herbal company, an MLM just down the street from us named Nature's Lab. I knew the owner. They were competitors of ours, just a small company. Dave said they were for sale. I thought this sounded great because I thought if I could buy a business that already had the products in place, that could work.

When I knocked on the door, the owner answered, a true one-man show, and I said, "I heard you want to sell your business."

He looked at me, a little stunned, and said, "I don't want to sell my business. But while you're here, come on in and we'll talk about it."

He said, "I'm not selling." So I went in and twenty minutes later I owned his business.

So I went in and twenty minutes later I owned his business. I had to go borrow money for it because my other businesses had eaten up my capital. I got a $20,000 loan and bought the business. He was doing $10,000 a month when I bought it. The company became Enrich International and when I sold it in 1997, it was doing $10 million a month in sales.

So these were the products that brought me back into the nutritional/MLM business. As we were growing that business, there were times where I found myself again thinking, *Maybe*

I was speaking at the Bally Hotel in Las Vegas at
an Enrich International Convention in the late '80's

it's time to exit. As soon as my thoughts traveled down that road, there was that inevitable invisible hand of God again, pulling me back until it *was* time to exit in 1997. I sold the controlling interest, then in 2000 I sold the rest of my shares in the company.

I was out of the industry with more money than I ever thought I'd have as a poor little boy living in California. Throughout these years, I also had my hand in multiple other businesses, and it fed my desire for new and interesting challenges. These lessons learned from the experiences I had over this couple of decades, combined with those I'd developed on my mission and in the military, plus being a husband and father, would serve me as I took on the next segment of my life's challenges led by the invisible hand of God.

CHAPTER 10

Spared . . .

O NE WOULD THINK that being in the Army my life might have been in peril, but I was never in a life-threatening situation there. I have had times in my life where I was close to death or thought something terrible might happen. Truthfully, I don't remember all of them, but I just know I've felt throughout all these years many times that God was intervening to spare my life.

In the Nature's Sunshine days, when we had the company airplane with two engines—I was a pilot at that time, which was more of a hobby than anything—I remember one of the times I was flying along with our pilot into Salt Lake City. The airport traffic control had me on final approach. As we descended to land, all of a sudden in front of us was a commercial jet sitting on the runway ready to take off, and we were about to land right on top of it. I missed it and went around. That incident didn't scare me as much as it startled me because the controller in the tower had told me to land and we were on their radar.

One time in a blizzard in Toronto, Canada we had enough visibility to take off, but it was a dark night and snowing heavily. The tower told us to taxi out to the runway and get ready to take off, but just as we pulled onto the runway, a big commercial jet touched down probably no more than 25 to 50 feet in front of us. It could have landed right on top of us and we would never have seen it or known what happened. That was one of those experiences when I know my life was spared, no question.

It's an unsettling feeling to wonder if your time is up. One morning in 1997, Linda was getting ready to go to the airport and fly to Louisiana to visit her family to meet up with some of her siblings. She caught the plane and was en route. I hadn't told her that I wasn't feeling well, but when I got up that morning, I'd had a heaviness in my chest and thought, of course, it would go away.

I've always been healthy, so I honestly wasn't concerned. I got in my car to drive to work and about mile up the road I had tingling in my arms. I wondered if I was actually having a heart attack and said a prayer to ask God if I should go to the hospital or if this would pass and turn out to be nothing serious. I felt I needed to go to the hospital. The whole time I had a heavy chest and now the tingling in my arm, so I walked into the ER and told the receptionist I thought I was having a heart attack.

They took me right in and laid me on a table. The ER doctor came in immediately and, sure enough, I was having a heart attack. They gave me nitroglycerin and asked me what my pain level was on a scale of 1 to 10, with 10 being the worst. And at that time I said, "Well, about a 2." I'm pretty tolerant of pain and can take quite a bit of it. So a 2 to me might have been a 5 or 6 to someone else.

The doctor gave me some more pills and drugs and all of a sudden my pain shot up to about an 8. I got a little bit panicky and really thought I was going to lay there and die. I told the doctor the pain was an 8 and she suggested we just wait for a minute to see what would happen. A few seconds later the pain started to subside. She told me the heart attack was caused by a clot and she'd given me a blood thinner to dissolve it. In the process of doing that the pain level will typically go way up, and then goes way down. Which it did.

> I really thought I was going to lay there and die.

Luckily I didn't have to have open heart surgery. The doctor did do an angiogram the next day and saw some blockage in the vein behind my heart. That vein has never been known to cause a heart attack but they used a balloon to open it up anyway. They didn't find any more blockage in my arteries at that time. That was another experience where I felt that I was spared.

I was fifty-two when this happened. My father had a massive heart attack at sixty-seven and ended up having open heart surgery. A third of his heart muscle was completely dead. They removed that part and told me they'd never had a patient survive with that much damage to the heart. But my father was spared and never even had to take any medications the rest of his life. The surgeon said Dad would just get up one day and drop dead, that his heart would just stop. He lived almost twenty more years. *His* own father, my grandfather, had a heart attack at sixty-seven which actually killed him. Heart attacks run in my family so I felt very fortunate that I survived. Had my grandfather had an opportunity for open heart surgery and the advancements we have now, he might have lived.

It's always interesting to me after the fact that the invisible hand of God has worked in so many ways in my life. It's guided and protected me, steered me in certain directions, and spared me. I believe it's this way for all of us—the trick is recognizing it for what it is.

Feeling as though mortality might be coming to an end can cause some deep pondering. Those times force me to truly think of the things that matter most, to consider those aspects of life that provide the most richness, the things I can do to make life better for those around me. Certain parts of my existence come into sharp focus.

When my life's work is boiled down to its essence, the times when I am most satisfied are when I can see myself growing and achieving more, and all in conjunction with helping my family, other people, and providing jobs. When I'm creating or buying businesses, seeing them expand, or seeing people in Zija, in particular, become successful, I feel real joy. Some of these people have never experienced success in their lives—now they're on stage receiving an award or they have achieved a higher rank. When I see how their lives have been blessed, *I feel blessed.*

"Aha" moments can come even when times are the hardest. In the mid to late '80s, I lost everything. At the end of it, I filed for bankruptcy, not because I wasn't going to pay the debt off, but because I wanted to keep the phone from ringing from creditors until I could take care of them. I went back and repaid all of the debt. I refused to leave anyone hanging if I knew about them.

I had no net worth at that time. I did have a job and was making a little bit of money—it was in the early days of Enrich International. One night I had a dream. In this dream, which I believe was inspired, I was shown that my responsibility in life was to create employment and help people. And in that process, God was going to give me a tremendous amount of wealth, far more than I'd experienced before.

Now I'm seeing the fulfillment of that in my life. I woke up and told Linda and my parents about the dream because it was very powerful to me, to feel that things were going to change from having nothing to being blessed with an abundance that would create so many jobs for people in so many businesses that I own now.

> After this particular dream, I looked at what I was doing in a different light.

Before that dream I'd always created jobs—Nature's Sunshine created jobs, my other publishing company did too—everything I did seemed to create jobs, but I never thought of them in terms of the importance of that. I just saw that you have to create jobs in order to become successful and to make something work. But after this particular dream, I looked at what I was doing in a different light.

One of my purposes is to create employment for people, for God's children, to help bless their lives. I now look at people who are working with me or for me, whether they're my children, distributors, direct employees, whether it's in Zija or one of my other companies, and I see these people as being an important part of my mission in life. That's where my focus has to be. I talk a lot now about nutrition, especially with my distributors—how they bless the lives of people nutritionally. I tell them to not worry about the money. The money will follow. And it's rather like that for me, too. If I create enough jobs in my companies, the money will take care of itself. It always has. I've always had a skill and a knack for making money. I've always have been able to take care of my family, but now my focus has to be on not just making money, although you have to make money or you can't make jobs, but on creating employment for people and helping them do better than they think they can.

CHAPTER 11

You Saw More in Me
Than I Saw in Myself . . .

I WAS A LATE BLOOMER with church responsibilities. Later in life I was assigned to be a bishop in the LDS church, the equivalent of a pastor, and I was responsible for more than six hundred members. I learned to love the people, to put them first. I experienced this on a different level than ever before, helping people with their family life, helping them financially, and counseling those who had challenges with their faith.

When I was released as bishop to take another church calling, I gathered all my leaders together for a testimony meeting. I told them I didn't want the meeting to be about me, I just wanted to hear their testimonies about their church service, their lives, and Christ. There was a man in this group who was very much like I had been many years before. He was quiet, not a natural leader. He said, "When I accepted this position, I felt very inadequate for the job. But I did it, and not only that, I've excelled far beyond what I thought I could do. I thank you, Bishop, because you expected more out of me. You saw more in me than I saw in myself."

I've thought back to that statement many times through the years since. It could have been any bishop, it wasn't just that it was me or my efforts with this man. But isn't that the responsibility of a leader? To expect more out of their people than they think they can give? It's not that people *can't* do it, they just don't see it in themselves. I've accomplished so much more than I ever imagined, but I couldn't see this potential in myself when I was a teen, a young man. It's as if I had to experience all of these other things first to rise up.

> It's not that people *can't* do it, they just don't see it in themselves.

We can always do more. Sometimes we need a mentor there who can see more in us, to help us rise up and accomplish those things we never imagined doing. The mentors in my life began, of course, with my parents, and then progressed naturally to my bishop in Bakersfield, mission presidents, my wife, and children, Jack Ritchason, and many others.

My temporal blessings have allowed me to give back to the incredible spiritual community that raised me. It has been my privilege to share a portion of what I have with various projects for the church, and in so doing, I met a man who has not only been a mentor to me, but also a dear friend.

M. Russel Ballard is one of the Apostles of my church and has been a close, personal friend for over twenty years. We bonded, even though he's sixteen years my senior. He's a great man who has the love of Christ and all the gifts that I imagine a great spiritual leader to have. He possesses a sincere love for his fellow man and expects the very best that people have to offer.

We formed a friendship when I was invited to his office at the suggestion of a mutual acquaintance, Steve Studdard, who had worked on President Ronald Reagan's staff. I met Steve while taking a tour of the United Nations in New York. Steve happened to be the leader of that tour. He had this incredible ability to always remember people's names and something about them once introduced to him.

Steve introduced me to Russ Ballard—in our church we call him "Elder Ballard"—because the church was gathering support from private individuals for the "This is the Place Monument and Park" in Salt Lake City. It's a sample "settlement" or town honoring the pioneers and the way they lived. It's called Deseret Village. You can actually see homes, stores, newspaper offices, and the like from the 19th century. Elder Ballard asked me to help with one of these replicas of a building from the 1800's. It was actually a drug store. I was happy to do that and dedicated the little building to my grandparents because they were pioneers in Utah—also because I loved them very much and wanted to honor them.

Whenever there has been a need in the church above and beyond tithing, I've always wanted to share what I have because I've felt that my money was given to me by God and it's His to use any way He sees fit.

The friendship I formed with Elder Ballard bonded us further the more we talked. I shared that my grandfather, William Frederick Webster, had served a mission for the

church under a mission president named Melvin J. Ballard—
Elder Ballard's grandfather. So my grandfather was a
missionary with his grandfather in the northwestern states of
the United States.

Elder Ballard was also a businessman before he became a
church leader, so because of my business background, about
every three months or so he would invite me to his office
in Salt Lake City and we would visit for about an hour,
sometimes on religious topics, sometimes on business. He
was always interested in how my businesses were doing. It
has been a true joy to get to know him better through the
years and I cherish that friendship.

The ties we have with people often have their roots,
as I mentioned, with our relatives or ancestors. There was
a further tie to Elder Ballard, interestingly enough, again
with my maternal grandfather. He was the Stake President
of an area in south central Utah, called Wayne County. A
Stake President has responsibility for all of the members,
including their bishops, in a certain area. My grandparents
lived in a town called Loa where they often hosted church
General Authorities (the top leaders of the church) in their
homes when those leaders came to the area for meetings with
church members. As a young girl, my mother remembered
that Melvin J. Ballard stayed in their home and related an
experience of his when Christ appeared to him right before he
was called as an Apostle. Experiences like this are truly sacred
and seldom talked about in the church. My mother told me
that story when I was a teenager, so this was an additional tie
I felt with his grandson, M. Russell Ballard.

Church service continued for Linda and me. In 2002, we were called to serve a mission together in Atlanta, Georgia for a period of eighteen months. We worked with young people more as peers than as leaders and what a great experience it was to be with my companion, my wife, on a 24/7 basis. It truly was a choice time to grow together, to bond and learn to love the young missionaries, love the people we served, to cry with them when they cried, to help pull them up.

Linda and I worked with this wonderful single man by the name of Darrell. We grew to love Darrell so much. Even though he had so many challenges in life, he was a wonderful guy. But he had a serious problem. He was a bold-faced liar. He was a person who, I believe, managed to convince himself that his lies were truth. It was driving me insane, so I told Linda one night, "Darrell's coming over for dinner and I'm going to drop a bomb on him. I'm going to tell him I'm not putting up with his lies anymore." She was concerned he'd never come over again.

Dinner time came and Darrell with it. I took the bull by the horns and told him, "Darrell, you are a bold-faced liar. Everything that comes out of your mouth is a lie. And I'll tell you what, God doesn't like liars. And I don't either."

Now I've expressed my beginnings as an introverted, shy person. But through the years, I became very bold. I think you have to be bold and able to speak your mind. When you do it with love, you *can* be bold with them. I learned that from my mother and I'm not half of what she was. She had such an amazing ability that if someone around her said or did something wrong, she could chew them out, up one side

> She could chew them out, up one side and down the other, and they would thank her for it and love her all the more.

and down the other, and they would thank her for it, and love her all the more. She did it with a smile on her face and somehow it worked. Most people can't do that.

I learned that from her, but I'm not as good at it; however, I suppose I inherited enough of that talent because Darrell just sat there and looked at me for a minute, and I think he ended up loving me all the more because he knew I cared about him enough to be honest with him. He thanked me, made his sandwich for dinner, and he kept coming back.

Darrell was a bright man with a good heart and the potential for success. One time he ran out of gas and called and asked if I'd loan him five bucks. So I went to the gas station and said I was going to fill his tank up. But I said, "I want you to do two things. One, don't ever call and ask me for gas money again. And two, when your gauge gets to half full, fill it up. It doesn't cost any more money to fill it on the top end." He never called and asked for gas money again. He'd learned to fix the problem. He'd learned a principle.

It takes boldness sometimes to help people and Darrell knew right where I stood. People can learn and change if they want to. There was more to Darrell than he saw in himself. He has improved his life so much, his standard of living, everything. It has been such a pleasure to see his success. He's worked hard and I know he's doing better financially.

Darrell learned how to keep God's commandments, and he learned some basic success principles, and how to follow them. It's always been interesting to me to see how religious principles and basic life and success principles go hand-in-hand. A combination of these beliefs played a big part in our mission in Georgia. How do you become a stronger person if you call someone up and ask for five bucks and then never repay them? Just like the big kid in junior high who never repaid my quarter and then avoided me altogether. I'd rather have someone say, "Can you *give* me five bucks." I'll do that. But it's better if people learn to be self-sufficient. I learned that principle at a really young age, asking my dad for a candy bar, and I'm lucky that my children are that way. They stand on their own feet. Anyone can do it if they'll just apply the principles that lead to success.

It's harder at some times than other times. When we hit bottom, we pick ourselves up. That's okay. I don't think anyone goes through life with a silver spoon in their mouth. Even if you start with one, you may lose it and have to figure out a way to put it back in your mouth. And thankfully we can do hard things—because there's often more to us than we can see in ourselves.

CHAPTER 12

Multi-Tasking at Its Finest . . .

A FTER OUR MISSION TO GEORGIA, Linda and I returned home and were both received leadership positions in our church. We conducted missionary training in the Missionary Training Center in Provo, Utah for "senior couples," as we had been trained. We taught them how to help people make commitments and keep them. I've seen the overlap with my business life because this also applies to the MLM industry—how do you get people to commit to something and then keep that commitment? That's a big challenge.

In late 2004, Dave Andrews, the former CFO of one of my previous companies, called me with a business proposition he wanted me to review. I knew he wanted to start another MLM business and I knew he wanted my money to do it. Because he was who he was, I agreed to hear him out. I even told David Shurtliff, who worked for me at the time, "I'll give him thirty minutes and then tell him nicely 'thank you, but it's not for me right now.'"

Dave arrived for the appointment with a thick stack of papers that I really did not want to read. But rather than shove the papers at me, he asked instead if he could show me a video. I liked that option a lot better. He showed me a Discovery Channel Special highlighting the moringa plant, which was shown to have health properties that were really amazing. Every minute of that video, I felt the invisible hand of God pulling me and telling me I needed to be involved in this venture, to help his children all over the world have access to this incredible resource. I had actually seen that God wanted this product to bless the lives of His children nutritionally throughout the world.

I had some stipulations, however. I told Dave I didn't want to run the day-to-day operations and I would put up the money but wanted to keep the controlling interest in the company. He agreed, so we got to work.

We worked eight long months to develop the product. How on earth do you turn a tree into a drink? We needed to know the best sources for the plant. Once we had access to that, we had to determine how best to develop the product itself. Again, it's not a juice in its natural state. This is a *tree*. We had to nutritionally balance the formula so the product had all the nutrition possible in the drink, which meant the right locations, the right soil, the right plant, the right conditions . . . it was a huge task.

Our formulator, Russ Bianchi, whom we hired to develop the drink, ran 133 tests and all of them failed. Not quite as bad as Edison with his 5,000 attempts at the light bulb, but 133 fails tried Russ's patience. He was ready to throw in the towel when his wife told him he couldn't quit after spending our money on the endeavor. She told him he'd better figure out a way to make it work. So he went back and ran the test eleven more times and got it.

We had a product ready to go! Again I saw the invisible hand of God making it work, because it almost *didn't* work. But to turn that into a drink, that invisible hand of God had to be present and confirmed the vision I had when I saw that video.

The tricky part for Linda and me was that we'd been called to serve full-time again in the church. But this time I was asked to be a mission president in South Carolina for *three years*. I knew when Dave approached me that this was in the works and I'd have only eight months to get this new business up and running before heading out the door. But we had our product, we had the staff hired, and the compensation plan in place, and the beginnings of a distributor force, so all was well.

We'd been in South Carolina for about six weeks when I got a phone call at about eight o'clock one night from Ann Pyne, who worked for me. I'd left her and David Shurtliff in charge of Zija to make sure my investment was okay for the three years while I was gone. She told me Dave Andrews had a massive heart attack and was dead. There I sat 2,000 miles away, wondering what on earth I was going to do.

> There I sat 2,000 miles away, wondering what on earth I was going to do.

I'd made a commitment and I wasn't going to leave South Carolina. But I had responsibilities to the company, to all the employees, the distributors, the scope was huge. I told Ann to visit Kathy, Dave's wife, after the funeral and buy the shares back from her. Ann sat down with Kathy and negotiated an agreement with her so that she'd be financially secure, which she is and will be until the day she dies. She was well compensated. I got the shares back which I had to have and ran the company from a distance. For three years.

It was a challenge. And the crazy thing was every month or two, Ann would call and say, "Ken, the company's doing better, sales are going up! We need you to send another hundred thousand dollars."

What? How does that work? So I'd send a check. Then a month or so later, Ann would call again and say, "Ken, sales are going up! We need you to send two hundred thousand dollars."

Sales were going up and I had to send even more money? I knew there were some problems there and I said, "Ann, maybe I ought to just pull the plug on this thing. If it keeps going like this, it's going to bankrupt me."

She said, "Ken, I promise if you stay put, everything is going to work out. It's a great product, people love it, miracles are happening."

So I said, "Okay, here's the two hundred."

One month the amount she needed reached as high as $250,000. Every time I got those crazy calls it just drove me insane. Two or three times I said, "Ann, maybe I should pull the plug on this," but it's like that invisible hand of God was there and wouldn't let me pull the plug! I stayed in, Ann was confident that the product was remarkable, and the day that my three-year commitment was up, I went home. The first thing I did was walk back into the corner office where accounting was and said, "You will not spend one more dollar unless I authorize it." After that, the losses started dropping and about eight months later, Zija was finally a success. Sales were going up and the company has been profitable ever since.

In the middle of all that, of course, I was a mission president with responsibilities for over four hundred young people in their early twenties over that three-year period. And it was truly a great experience. I was able to teach them everything I'd learned, where I put together those skills that make for not only great missionary work, but great business dealings. The trick was to teach it to these good kids, and not only that, but to get them to do it over and over and over again. To teach it so that it became a success habit for them. And it did. Our success rate, looking at the numbers again, because I'm a numbers person, more than doubled in that three-year period. This was very rare and it was significant, not because of me, but because of a few concepts I was able to share and help people learn.

Again, boldness is one of these things and it's a valuable life lesson for everyone. Don't be afraid to be bold! As it applied to missionary work, we taught the missionaries to teach people to make commitments and then follow up. You have to follow up. How do you get people to come to church when they say they will and then they don't?

I sat down with a couple of missionaries and a lady once.

> Don't be afraid to be bold!

The missionaries' goal was to get her to commit to come to church. I listened as they conversed and she said, "Yeah, I'll come to church Sunday."

I looked at her and said, "No you won't. You're lying to us," just like that, with a big smile on my face, thinking of my mother. And because this woman knew I cared about her, she just sat back stunned for a second because who tells someone they're lying in this day and age?

She said, "You know, you're right. I am lying and I won't do it again. But I'm not coming to church Sunday." The relationship wasn't damaged, the message was delivered in good humor and sincerity, and rather than keep this woman in a position where she'd continue making commitments she was never going to follow through on, everything was out in the open.

If you love people, you can be bold with them, as long as you've got a big smile on your face and let them know you care about them. They've got to know you care. I can't stress it enough. If you love people, they can take challenges like that and they learn. Just like Darrell. He didn't lie to me ever again and I believe he's tried to make honesty a part of his life. If I hadn't been bold with him, he'd still be lying and unable to move past the consequences of that.

Why aren't people bold? How do we overcome that reluctance? We are always afraid of offending somebody. It's hard. We don't want to offend people. In reality, there are many who would rather have the truth spoken straight to them, than find out after the fact that you weren't bold at the risk of being offensive. There are people who find out later on that you were going along with their story, not because you believed it, but because you were worried about being rude. How unfortunate and sad would it be to realize you could have made a difference if you'd been brave enough to help someone make a course correction, kindly and with love?

I believe we're put on this earth to help each other. Bold does not mean cruel. You don't have to be mean, in fact you shouldn't be mean. But it's a double-edged sword. We also have to realize when we point a finger out—even if it's justified or necessary—that there are three fingers pointing back at *us*. We'd better make sure if we're telling someone not to be a liar that *we're* not a liar. See what it takes to be bold? Whatever it is you're telling them not to do, you'd better not be doing it either, or they'll see hypocrisy. If that's how you are, it will destroy that relationship. Honesty and integrity must accompany boldness. No hypocrisy. Love unfeigned. It's hard and takes a lot of time and effort. But it's crucial and it's worth it.

CHAPTER 13

Lessons Learned . . .

We're all a composite of our ancestors. Their genetic makeup is part of us and I believe it influences us to a certain degree. I had a genealogist research my family once and she said "You have more pilgrim ancestry in your veins than anyone I've ever researched." I think many Americans who have been here for very long probably have some relationship to that group. I've always had an affinity toward the pilgrims. They sacrificed everything. Some even sacrificed their lives. They came here for freedom. I think that's part of the human condition, the yearning and need for freedom. I want to be able to do what I want to do as long as I don't hurt other people.

My grandfather, William Frederick Webster, my mother's father, was a quiet man but he was very successful in his life. Those genes from him must have imprinted themselves pretty firmly into my makeup, because I patterned my business life after his more than any other person. He lost his mother when he was six and his father was extremely busy on the farm. At the age of eight, my great-grandfather told my grandfather, "You're on your own. You have to provide for yourself."

From that day forward he worked, providing for himself and then later for his family. He started out as a sheep herder and went up in the mountains in the summer with some other rough and tumble old sheep herders. At night they'd sit around the campfire and talk. My grandfather was given the assignment to cut their chewing tobacco plugs for them. He didn't start chewing, but he would lick his blade clean after he cut the plugs. That eventually led to him acquiring a habit of chewing tobacco himself. I don't know when he gave it up, certainly way before I ever came into the picture.

When he was twenty-one, he married my grandmother, who was sixteen. He continued working hard and by that time, not only was he completely independent, but he owned a ranch with cattle and horses, had his own horse and buggy, and owned his own home. He grew up in very poor, desperate circumstances which probably drove his ambition to provide for himself and be a success. My grandmother grew up in even more dire circumstances. Later in life she wouldn't even take us to where she'd grown up as a little girl because she was embarrassed by it. Her family had been so painfully poor.

Grandpa Webster went on to start the first two movie theaters in town and was a half-owner of them. He got rid of them when he found out his partner was cheating and stealing money from the company. He couldn't deal with dishonesty. I think his influence made a huge impact on me and my own feelings about honesty.

He started the only five-and-ten cent store in town. He owned a freight company that he actually ran himself between a few of towns. He started it out with a couple of horses and a trailer. By the time automobiles came along, he was able to get his own truck to haul with which made the trip faster. He also was a twenty percent owner of the bank in town that he and four other men started up. He was very successful in business, was always making money, but was always very generous and would give money to anyone who asked. He even invested in some foolish things just because people asked him to.

Grandpa Webster was always successful. When he lived in Wayne County, Utah, where he lived until he retired, he was the wealthiest man in the county. I'm not entirely certain what that word means because I don't think anybody was wealthy in those days or had a lot of money—it was all relative, I'm sure. But his home had the first indoor plumbing in the whole county. This is where my mother and her siblings were born. She learned frugality and hard work from both her parents, but especially her father.

My paternal grandfather, John Henry Brailsford, was a mentor to me as well. He ran away from home at thirteen and went to the coal mines in Utah where he worked until he was hurt in a coal mine disaster. He then went to work for JC Penny as one of their first employees, grew up in that organization, and was successful. When he retired he had a large block of JC Penny stock.

These stories drive me on. I love to read about people's successes, especially when it's about my own ancestors. I believe that when we read about other people, we can be motivated by their successes. If we just think, "Look, if that person can do it, so can I!" then the sky's the limit.

"Look, if that guy can do it, so can I!"

I find it interesting now to see that the business gene has traveled down through me and into my own grandkids. When I was young, when my homework was done, I would sit and play board games if there were no friends around. I loved the games "Easy Money," "Monopoly," and "Risk." Those were my three favorites. I played all six characters and I always won, of course. I learned the tricks of the trade through those games. Even to this day I've never been beaten in Monopoly.

My grandson, Harrison Cutler, thirteen years old at the time, was extremely good at Monopoly. He challenged me one day and I said, "Well, you're going to lose."

I loved tubing with the kids in the mountains behind Springville, Utah

He said, "No I'm not. I don't lose."

So I said, "Let's see." We played the board game and he was tough to beat, *but I did beat him.* He was somewhat depressed, but I was proud of him and glad to see that same fascination for business and making money in him. I haven't wanted to play him since because I think now he *would* probably beat me!

Sometimes the best of training, the best education, the best of everything life has to offer to prepare us for our vocation will fall short and we will stumble. It's part of the mortal experience and, although painful, the struggles sometimes teach us the most valuable lessons.

In addition to the businesses I've created, I've also bought several already in existence. For the most part, they've been successful. But my biggest disappointment in business was a mining venture. I had a partner and we had a mine in Colorado that in the 1890's had been a successful copper and silver mine. It had produced roughly 500,000 ounces of silver. We started to mine it, took the shaft deeper into the vein of ore, and began to buy equipment to extract the silver and a little bit of gold. We struggled with it, mainly because neither of us knew what we were doing.

We spent probably a million dollars developing that mine over the course of a year or two and had what we thought should produce the ore. We knew that there was silver in the ore, we didn't care so much about the copper, but we could never get a process that would separate the silver from the other metals in the rock. We never turned it into a profitable venture. I felt really bad about it and lost a lot of money. A lot of other investors had lost their money as well. I felt terrible.

About the same time we were working on the mine, we bought a placer gold mine near the Arctic Circle in Alaska. We did produce gold there and were successful, but we could never make it profitable and could only run part of the year. We had to pay the guys a lot of money to be up there— their airfare, lodging and food, etc.—and I really think that it could've been profitable, but because the gold was free-form gold, some of it, maybe a lot of it, was stolen by different employees. So we never saw it. Unfortunately, that taught me to really watch employees more closely because you can't always trust people. They'll think of themselves first rather than think of making the company a success. People need to understand that if their company is not successful, *their own careers and jobs will not last.*

We had some property in the Yukon that was gold-bearing which we never put into production. At a certain point, I threw in the towel on that because I knew that without huge amounts of money we could never make it profitable. Not only that, you need the right geologists and engineers to know how to extract the precious metals and turn the operation into a productive mining property. So these were big failures in my business life. But they taught me that not every venture is successful. Sometimes you're going to experience failure.

Many years later, I reflected back on my prior business dealings in publishing. I had a good knowledge base to work from and knew how that industry operated. I found a religious book publishing company that was struggling and I wanted help them. This company was losing money and they didn't have good financial statements.

There were two mistakes with this venture—one my fault, one the circumstances. I jumped into that business and threw money at it before I knew the total mess they were in from the financial statements. Once I realized that, it became the first thing I would do in future businesses. I had to make sure the financial statements were good. You have to know where you are at all times. I never go more than a month without a financial statement.

In this particular publishing company, when we finally got the financial statements straightened out, I realized the problems went much deeper than I expected so I had to cut some people. I didn't like doing that. They were good people. But I couldn't sustain the company with them. I really tightened the screws on expenditures, bringing the costs down, getting it close to breaking even, but not totally there, still having to put money into it.

At the same time, the industry changed to e-books. I thought we had three to five years to get our back list converted into e-books. But the trend moved so fast that it actually took just a year until more than half of the books in the country being sold were e-books. We weren't prepared for that and it pushed us into a deeper financial hole.

I could see there was no way to dig us out of it, so I closed the business down and took my losses. Whenever I've done that, I've always paid every debt on the books. I don't file bankruptcy as a rule—I just pay all of the debts owed and close the business down. I don't believe in letting people hold the bag for my mistakes. Even if I didn't have the money, I'd find a way to pay it. The biggest lesson I learned with this experience was to research and do my homework. The best advice I can offer anyone buying a struggling company is to be careful and don't buy it unless you know exactly what the financial statements say. It's better not to do it at all.

Everything I've learned throughout my life has brought me to this point. If I had missed any of those experiences, how would that have changed my course? I can see where God has brought me here—in my business life, my family life, my spiritual life. Where would I be if I'd taken another path? God took a boy born into a family of humble circumstances, an introvert who had a hard time talking to people, and turned him into the person I am now.

CHAPTER 14

The Underdog Dilemma . . .

I ALWAYS WANTED A SIBLING SO BADLY I think I drove my parents nuts saying, "When am I going to have a brother?" Add to that, I was short and worried a lot about it when I was younger. These things were a big deal to me at the time. I have a grandson now who's short. He'll probably end up being about my height. So I know what he will be going through. When you experience this kind of stress (and many other kinds) as a kid, it can be daunting. And perception is reality. Those things that may seem like no big deal to adults can be crucial to kids.

Unfortunately, life really doesn't get any easier as you grow older. But hopefully as adults, we can reason through our challenges and make some decisions, some choices. When we find ourselves in that "underdog" place, we can either let it knock us down and keep us down, or we can say, "I'm going to overcome this." These decisions will determine our destiny.

So many people say, "Oh, pity me. Why did God do this

to me?" To which I say, "Blah, blah, blah." God didn't do anything to you and if you don't help pull yourself up, you may as well have done it to yourself. You have agency, you choose. If you want to get back up, God will help you pull yourself up. People around you will help. You'd be surprised how many people will rally and help if you have the right attitude.

That was the attitude I always took. When I was on the bottom while others were succeeding, I thought if so-and-so can do this, I can do it too! I am happy to see people excel, even my competitors in business. I'm happy if they excel as long as they leave me alone to go after them and compete the best I can. I've never given a lot of attention to what my competitors are doing. I only care about what I'm doing. Am I doing the best? If I see a competitor doing better than me, I think, "Look, they're not any smarter than I am. We're going to go after them and do better!" I'm happy that they're there. They help lead the way and help blaze the trail.

So go after it with everything you have. That's what you do when you become the underdog. You pick yourself up and move forward. The invisible hand of God is so real in our lives, whether we realize it or not. I'm here today because of that invisible hand. I know I was prepared for it all the way through. There are so many instances throughout my life that brought me to where I am right now, in the religious realm, material realm, worldly realm, all of it. When you get on this side of your life and look back and think about it, you can start to see those miracles from His hand.

It is important that we do what we were sent here to do. What is your responsibility? You must decide what you're going to be part of and you can do it. What role you play depends on you and how you've been prepared. Not everyone's going to do the exact same thing in life, but that's the beauty of it. I think we can all do amazing things if we want to strongly enough. There's a lot of good to do and we *can* do it.

The positions I've had with MLM companies in the past, and especially now with Zija International, required that I get up in front of people and speak—a lot. I can't get up and read a scripted talk. I'd put everyone to sleep. I have to talk from my heart and hope to motivate and inspire people. Everything that has brought me to this point in my life affects people all around me, whether in business or family. The ripples in my life affect you, just as the ripples in your life affect me and everyone else.

> I think everyone can do amazing things if they want to strongly enough.

I do not believe in coincidences. I believe God leads us through life to where He needs us to be to serve His purposes. We might think they're our purposes, and they become our purposes, but they're His first. So He gives us experiences and contact with people we need to get us where we need to end up.

We get beaten up our whole lives—sometimes physically, but certainly most of us have been emotionally battered by life. Sometimes it can be family saying, "You can't do that. You shouldn't do that. I don't know why you'd do that." Or perhaps a classmate at school puts us down, making us feel less than we are.

> We have to believe in ourselves and throw those shackles off.

We can all probably relate to that. But we have to believe in ourselves and throw off those shackles. We cannot allow ourselves to be bound down by disbelief in our own abilities *because we are children of God*—His sons and daughters, and as sons and daughters of God, we can do everything that He wants us to do. That's why He has His invisible hands in our lives, to help us accomplish the things He wants us to do.

I know this because He's done it in my life and I'm no different than you. You're as good as I am and I'm as good as you are. We have to know that just because someone's up on a stage, it doesn't make them better than we are. Don't ever let anyone make you feel that way. We are all given different assignments by God to accomplish different things in life. Because we come and take on this physical body, we don't remember that time with God before we came here, but if we could, I firmly believe we'd realize that we accepted our life's challenges before we came. I know it.

Now it's our job to find out what our purposes are. The things we do every day can bless God's children throughout the world. As I remind the Zija distributors, and this applies to anything in life, the money will take care of itself. Don't worry about the money. Get involved and love the people you work with. Teach them and share your gifts with them. You will find yourself blessed in ways you never imagined.

When I go back and look at my life, where I began, I really am amazed. I was not from a rich family. I had very frugal parents who didn't waste money. I'll always remember that time as a little boy, walking across the street and holding my dad's hand, asking for a candy bar he couldn't afford to buy me. But I learned that I was smart enough and strong enough to figure things out for myself.

My dad was swindled out of that small skin care business. When I started Nature's Sunshine, he shook his head and said, "I don't think you can make any money doing this." But I didn't buy into that statement. It wasn't given to me maliciously, that was just his belief because of his experience. If I'd accepted his words as truth, where would I be today? You can become a product of negativity even when it's not intended sometimes.

As we started our manufacturing company with Enrich International, guess who my first two employees were? My parents. They were retired and worked for free for me, running the production. They supported me 100% as most of parents will, or should, just as we should with our children. I will forever bless their names because of that. They helped me. We help each other. We pull each other up. We don't step on each other.

There are no coincidences in life. God has His gentle, invisible hand in all we do, from the cradle to the grave. He loves us and tells us we are special because to Him, we truly are.

CHAPTER 15

What's It All For?

To SAY THAT THE MLM BUSINESS has changed through the years is an understatement. It was a $1,050 investment to start Nature's Sunshine, $25,000 to start Enrich International, and millions of dollars to start Zija International. It's not easy to get into and compete today, especially without any experience.

I've seen many things change. I've experienced wonderful things and heart-breaking things. But one of the most valuable lessons I've learned to date is this: be quick to forgive. I'll illustrate it with a story.

Some time ago, two of our top female distributors each had an opposing viewpoint. Whatever the outcome, one would not be happy. After much deliberation and prayer, I made up my mind. The leader, whose preference was not chosen immediately, came to see me at my office. She told me how stupid I was, that I knew nothing, and had made a very bad decision. Her four-letter words were worse than I had ever heard from any soldier while in the Army, and I had heard everything, or so I thought. I couldn't believe my ears!

I was speechless and just stood there dumbfounded. I can't remember how long she ripped into me, but it seemed like an eternity. She finally left, telling me she was through with the business. I never expected to see her again and heard nothing from her, as she was true to her word. She quit, along with some of her distributors.

About six months later, she returned to see me, apologizing for her bad language and wanting to resume her business again. Letting her know that I had already forgiven her and she was welcome back, she went on to explain why she had returned. She said, "I was so mad, my language was terrible, but you didn't say one word to me. You just let me yell and swear at you. Had you said one word, which you were fully justified in saying, I would not be here today."

I learned a valuable lesson that day: never permit another person to make you angry or react negatively to them. Be quick to forgive, even if they don't return. That is important in life as well as in business. It will make you a better leader and you'll be respected by others.

CHAPTER 16

Some Final Thoughts . . .

IN THE END, IT IS NOT THE AMOUNT OF MONEY you have made and accumulated in life, nor how many assets you have, that matters much. It is not how many and from whom you have received accolades or what praises have been sung about your life that counts. They are like a breeze in the heat of summer. Those cool breezes are here one second, and then, just as quickly as they come, they vanish into thin air. It is rather about your relationship with God that matters most. Have you moved your life in harmony with God's will and commandments? In short, have you become more Christ-like? What about your relationship with your family? Have you been their mentor, care-giver, leader, and most of all, have you truly loved and cared about them? Do they love you in return, honor and cherish you as their parent or relative? What about your fellow-man? Have you lifted all the downtrodden you could? Have you inspired them to do better and have they become better because of your friendship and association with them?

In short, have you truly given of yourself in an unselfish way? Have you made the world a better place because you were here, however long or short that may be? To this end, I pray and work to achieve these ideals, realizing that I have been anything but perfect. After all, I'm just a human with all my weaknesses and foibles and mistakes I have committed. I always wanted to do my best and I pray that I can do much more good with whatever years I have left.

1983 Family Photo
Back row: Sheri, Ken, Linda, Kenny
Front row: Lisa, Steven, Becky, John

INTERVIEWS WITH MY ASSOCIATES

Amazing People in My Life . . .

I WOULD NOT BE WHERE I AM TODAY were it not for the influence of some pretty amazing people God has put in my path through this life, another clear sign of His invisible hand. What follows are some of their words about our journey together . . .

LINDA BRAILSFORD

Linda is Ken's wife. She spends much of her time doing church service and spending time with their grandchildren. She has been his greatest supporter, the mother of their six children, and grandmother to their grandchildren and great grandchildren.

I MET KEN when he was twenty-two and I was nineteen. We were both at the same junior college in Bakersfield, California. I met him in a class he was teaching and he asked me out. I declined because I was flying to Los Angeles for a date with someone else that weekend. So he tried again and asked me out another time. I think we went to another religion class he taught that night. That was when I decided he was the smartest man I had ever met.

Ken knew things I had never thought about in a religious way. I was in awe. I thought there's something to this guy and I should really consider dating him more seriously. Just seven months later, we were married.

I've never been nervous a day in my life with Ken. I've never worried about what he would do for a living or how we were going to support our kids. I never gave it a thought because I had that much faith in his ability to provide. I never, even though we went through hard times, had the feeling that we would go without. Not that we didn't have our trials in life, we did, but in that sense of earning money, I never worried about Ken.

I had so much faith in Ken that I spent my time raising my family. Ken was there as much as he could be and I enjoyed every minute of raising my kids. He, of course, enjoys every minute of his business, and I didn't butt in his business. But he was always there for the kids and me. I think in Ken's life, besides work, he enjoyed traveling with his family.

The number one thing I appreciate about Ken is he is always honest. Number two, he loves his grandkids. The most fun times he's had with them are just sitting and visiting with them, intellectually, and talking to them. He gives them advice, so they ask for it a lot. And he's always happy. I think I have seen Ken depressed maybe twice in his life. That's a good trait to have—to always look for the good in things and be happy no matter what your circumstance. He has always been happy. And I've often told him, "I could live in a tent with you and be happy."

I think we're both the type that the money doesn't matter so much as that we're together and things feel secure. He's always made me feel secure. Ken always makes me feel like everything is going to be okay. Even with the death of our oldest son, Kenny, I felt everything would be okay, because I couldn't have gone through that without Ken and my other children. He's just always made me feel that everything will be all right.

Ken likes to work. He gets quite bored if he has to stay home. He likes to come down to Arizona now that he's older and take a breath and get away from the rush, but his "taking a breath" means he'll answer a phone call and email. He always checks numbers; he's a numbers person. He's begun working more full-time with Zija recently, but that doesn't bother me. I think it's because Ken's worked so hard his whole life, I don't want to stifle his drive, and I know how bored he can be at home if he's home too much. He'll pace the floor, then all of a sudden he'll stop and say, "I've got an idea." So his mind never shuts off.

I don't think we're unique in any way apart from other families. I just think every family has their situations and they learn from their experiences in life. We've sure learned from ours. Ken will be the first one to tell you he's far from perfect, and he's made a lot of mistakes in his business careers, but he's learned from every one of them. He is really happy for other people to succeed, but he's just driven to build things, and in a sense, he's told me a lot of times he loves the fact that he can create jobs for people so they can provide for their families. He loves that part of building an empire more than anything. Actually now that Ken is *somewhat* retired, he's building businesses.

But I don't see Ken *really* retiring. It used to scare me a little bit, but now it doesn't. I just see him so happy that it makes me happy. He's not working as hard as he used to. He's not running a marathon. He's walking a race, and the race is only against himself.

He likes to tease and if I say something about his driving, it's almost a joke with us. He likes to look around when he drives and I'll say, "Ken, pay attention to the road," and he always has a comeback—that he *is* paying attention, and how he *can* look and still pay attention. So I just laugh and think, *Okay.* But he's always looking to see what's around him because he always looking at businesses that are coming or going. So when we go on trips, I like to drive so he can look. And he'll say, "Well, that building wasn't there; I wonder what they're doing there."

Ken has always loved all of my family. He's always loved to be *with* my family and I think it's because he's never had any brothers or sisters. He's had two close cousins in his life— David Shurtliff and Brent Ashworth. And he's been close to them. He just really loves family.

SHERI CUTLER

Sheri is Ken's oldest daughter. She most recently worked as Zija International's Human Resource Director. She resides in Draper, Utah with her husband, Scott, and their five children.

DAD HAD HIGH EXPECTATIONS of us. He instilled that in me and I wanted to make him proud. We were super close—I was closer to my dad than my mom—still to this day. Not that I don't love my mom, but there's something about being the first daughter. He would call me his little wiggle worm because when he came home from work late at night, the only time I would get to spend with him was when he would read the newspaper, lying on the carpet. I would wiggle under the paper to have those special moments with him. So I was definitely his wiggle worm and he will still call me that every once in awhile.

I feel like there have always been higher expectations of me than of the younger kids. I just felt like my parents had three kids and then three other kids—kind of like two families, even though we were all raised together, if that makes sense. They were definitely more lenient on the younger ones.

I think one thing that my parents taught us is unconditional love. Some of my siblings struggled when they were teenagers, but my parents never shut them out because they weren't making the best choices. They loved them through their mistakes, and they had an open door policy—call us anytime, we're here to help. And they still have that to this day. That's something I'm trying to pass down to my kids. You can be disappointed in your child in a choice that they've made, but if you're disappointed, and they don't think you love them, that is really hard on a kid. And my parents? That's something I learned from them and I've passed down to my kids.

My dad was very goal-driven and wanted to provide. Mom never had to work. He was always the breadwinner, which is really hard nowadays to have a single income. It seems like in most families, both parents are working. He's always provided, taking care of my mom and all the kids. Still to this day, Dad tries to help with each of us kids, whether we want to work and learn his business or do something else. I think that that's a positive.

The only negative is that it puts pressure on the one left home doing schoolwork and everything else with the kids. My mom had to do all that. But she's a trooper. Dad was traveling a lot because of business, and with six kids, I can attest to this since I have five, doing it alone is hard! But when he was home, Dad tried to have little moments together with us and tried to spend as much time as he could with each of us individually.

Even when Dad was traveling, I knew I could call him anytime and he would drop everything. He would even fly home if there was a problem. He would be right there with us, so I never felt like he made himself scarce or unavailable. I think he was the best father that I could have asked for and needed. I saw him drop everything for his parents and for us, his kids.

It's expensive having a family. I'm always looking at items that I'm buying or needing and different ways I might make it into a business because of Dad's influence. I haven't (because of my age and because I'm a mom) been able to get my ideas from the idea stage yet, but I've talked to my dad and my husband about it. I love business. My heart is really in MLM, because I grew up with it and that's all I know. I thrive on the conventions and meetings and rubbing shoulders with such good people who are out there trying to make a better world. Health and wealth—that's what life is all about—trying to make enough to provide for your family and have time for your family. I'm so glad my dad taught me that.

The thing about life with Ken (I go between calling him Ken and Dad because I worked with him) is when I was at work and distributors would come through, I would never say, "I'm Ken Brailsford's daughter." I would always introduce myself as Sheri Cutler. People would come back to me and say, "You never said you were Ken's daughter!" I have learned how to be professional and work and wanted to earn my own merits, not get them because I'm Ken's daughter.

Dad taught us that you put in your time. You work hard and you move up based on your own merits. I started six years ago, just part-time, because I wanted to be home with my kids. Then I decided when they were all in school and I had more time, that if there was an opening in Human

Resources (since I really like people and trying to make them happy), HR would be perfect for me. So I moved into HR and was an assistant for years before I moved up. That was all on my own merits.

Dad's known as the "father of herbal encapsulation," and I feel like my father's a rock star! That may sound funny to some people, but he truly is sought out; I never realized that until I got older. People want to rub shoulders with him. They want to learn from him.

I went to Tokyo, Japan with Dad, and even the way that they treated me was like royalty. I think that people really want to know what has made him so successful. He's an icon in the industry. I'm pretty proud of him. He's my hero!

When we were sick as kids, Dad would give us goldenseal. But if we couldn't swallow pills or capsules, he would open one (if you haven't tasted goldenseal, it has a nasty flavor) and put the goldenseal on honey and give it to us morning and night. I remember him doing that because I was so sick. Some dads would lose patience and say, "Just swallow this thing; I don't have time for this." He never did that. He was always trying to make it easier for us. Just loving and caring.

Dad loves reading. It's one of his favorite hobbies. But he also loves simple things like going out and feeding the fish on his lake. He calls it a lake; I call it a pond. But he loves going out and feeding the fish.

I remember high school. Kids never ate healthy and were always in a rush. But Dad would make our breakfast drink for us every morning. It was like a morning smoothie that he would put cottage cheese, fruit, and juice in it and say, "Okay, everyone has to drink it all before you go to school." What dad, especially one who was extremely busy, would take the time to make sure that his kids were getting the nutrition that they needed? My Dad. That's who.

JOHN BRAILSFORD

John is Ken's second son. He is the VP of Logistics and Purchasing for Zija International. He resides with his wife, Michelle, in Sandy, Utah. He and Michelle are the parents of eight children and several grandchildren.

MY DAD IS A HARD WORKER. He's honest. He has integrity. One of my fond memories was when he put my mom's shorts on and went sun tanning in the backyard. He went to take a nap. He thought they were his shorts but they were *really* short! Another time he put a pair of my mom's pants on and asked everyone what was going on when they laughed at him!

Most people know how passionate Dad is about the church and his faith. People would be surprised to know that he gives more money to the church than he's expected. He's helped the church do a lot of things that even my siblings don't know about. He's very generous.

Dad is great as a grandpa. He loves the grandkids. In fact, he's a *great-grandpa* to my grandkids.

Ken helped us start our lives. I call him "Ken" at work and keep it professional. I call him "Ken" away from work, too. Sometimes he answers faster than when he's called "Dad."

I've worked at Zija since 2009. I started in the warehouse part-time for six months. I even ran the ostrich ranch before KEB. I've worked for him since I was twenty.

He's such a smart businessman because he puts the business and his employees before himself as far as finances. He pays himself last. And he's smart with numbers.

I don't think he will ever retire. As long as he's physically and mentally able, he will still work. Even if he loses the physical part, he still will work. No one knows that he majored in economics instead of finance or business. He's been successful because he puts the company's needs first. A lot of people whose businesses fail pay themselves first.

As a father, the biggest thing I've taught my kids is that your word is your bond. You're the only one that can keep your word. I learned that from my dad.

LISA JANDA

Lisa is Ken's second daughter. She is currently attending nursing school. She, her husband, Mark, and their three children reside in Gilbert, Arizona.

I've always looked up to my dad and I thought it was awesome as a kid that he was in such high demand for everyone. I'm his daughter so when I see everyone wants to be around him, it's impressive. Here I get to live with him, be at home with him, up close and personal with him, and see him every day. I admire him so much. I saw him work hard and I just thought I was special because he was special.

There are so many lessons I learned from my dad. His work ethic particularly—working hard on what you want to achieve is the main one because he's worked hard all his life, and he continues to work hard for what he wants.

I also admire his compassion and love for others and his service. And I've learned from him that it doesn't matter what people's opinions are about you. Dad just worked hard and achieved what he wanted to achieve. He had dreams and he always achieved them. He taught me to not let anyone stop me but still have compassion for everyone around me.

Dad loves everyone and they love him. He has that quality about him, which is huge, and I know people sense that. He cares for people and wants everyone to succeed and be happy. That is so important to my dad.

Dad supports a lot of people. I've always admired that about him. People who struggle in life with money and just don't have the means to live life comfortably—he notices and cares. He's pretty private about helping people. That's not a surprise to many people, but it's always surprised me. I hear from people how generous he is with his money. He is not greedy. He's just willing to help people financially.

When I was in high school and we went for tithing settlement, Dad gave a large sum of money to the bishop. That was Christmas time and he requested that the bishop give the money to a family in the ward that needed it and to not tell them who it was from. He didn't want them to know that it was from him. He gives a lot anonymously. He doesn't want the glory. He just wants to help people.

I remember when he helped the "This is the Place" development in Salt Lake City. They remodeled it back in 2012 and Dad helped with one structure. A lot of individuals who had donated money had their names on it, but my dad wanted to be anonymous. He doesn't like his name plastered everywhere. His happiness is that he is doing it, he's helping. He doesn't need everyone to know that he is doing it. What this has taught me is to be generous and to help others. I don't need the glory either.

I missed having a closeness with the employees of Dad's businesses because I moved to Arizona. And I'm sorry I can't go to Zija events and hear Dad speak or get to know the distributors on that level. My siblings get to know them better because they get to go to all the events. Some of them are there at corporate, or have been there, so I do miss that part—knowing more of what's going on in the day-to-day. But I also realize that my life in Arizona with my family is important and I need to concentrate on them, as well as my schooling. I need to build my own legacy like Dad has built his. He tells me all the time he's proud of what I'm doing. He always lets me know.

I remember when I was in high school, Dad took me and Becky to Hawaii for a business trip. He went with a partner who had a daughter about our same age. I loved it because when you have six kids, your attention is divided with all six of them there, so with it just being Becky and me spending a week in Hawaii, we got all his attention! We had a really great time and got to see him work a little bit there. It was good to see that side of him with his partner.

Every summer we would go on vacations as a family and my Dad would drive. We had great times. We would go in our motor home, traveling along with our cousins sometimes. If we weren't doing that, we were driving to California. But just being at home and watching TV with him, snuggling with him, was great, too. We would watch his shows because we just wanted to be by him. Because he traveled a lot, there were a lot of times he was gone building his dreams and his businesses. But when he was home, he would put his business aside to spend time with us so we could just be with him.

Dad is a movie buff. We were always going to action movies and he would always want us to go. He's still like that! He loved movies, especially James Bond movies, so we would go a lot as a family.

A lot of times when we were kids, we would go on Sunday drives, and Dad would just want to be with his family. We would all get in the car and go to the mountains or go through neighborhoods just to look at the different styles of houses. He just wanted to spend some quality time with us. We didn't have cell phones, so people wouldn't be calling him. We didn't have the world interrupting us. I treasured those Sunday drives. He was a good dad. He wanted to be there and be with us.

My parents love each other and they would do anything for each other. I mean they still have their little arguments, like every couple does, but they have never been anything major, and Mom and Dad always make up after. When we were kids, they would never argue in front of us. They wouldn't fight and they put each other first before us kids.

My mom would make sure my dad would have what he needed, make sure he was fed and his needs were met, and then she would take care of us. And Dad would always make sure Mom was okay. And as they get older, they want to spend more time together. They are getting closer and closer as they're getting older.

My dad also made a point to take us to go visit his parents (my grandparents) at least once a week. He treasured visiting with them and making sure they were okay and that their needs were met. It taught me to treasure my relationship with *my* parents and make sure I stay in touch with them often.

BECKY PALMER

Becky is Ken's youngest daughter. She is a busy homemaker which allows her husband, Ryan Palmer, to work at Zija International. She and Ryan reside in Orem, Utah with their three children.

M Y DAD USED TO TAKE ME on a lot of his trips, so I remember traveling. He always said the best way to learn is to actually travel and see the world. So I had the privilege of growing up in the industry. I think I started working when I was sixteen in the summers. Dad taught us the value of work.

We were kind of his guinea pigs with medicine. All he had to do was say, "Hey Beck, this will clear up your skin," and I would take it! So it was good we grew up in that healthy environment. I got sick right out of high school for probably a year. Really, really sick. And my dad tried everything. We finally found a doctor that did IV's, so Dad would go with me and do it with me. He was always there. He was always willing to go and do whatever it took. That's probably the dearest story to me. He would do the drips, too. We would go together and that would just be our time. I know they were expensive, but that was our thing. He was sweet like that.

One of my fondest travel memories is of one of the times

we went to Hawaii. He took us to this island and this really nice resort. I remember that they did this obstacle course and my dad even did it. They were throwing baking flour over your head and it was so funny because he doesn't play much. But when he does, he really gets into it. That will always stick out in my memory. He is funny, he will joke and tease, but he is just so straight-laced that it is even funnier when he does it.

Another fond memory is when my dad went to Germany with me and my husband to do stem cell research for our son, Carson, who has Down Syndrome. Dad is busy but he makes the time for us. My parents have always been there for us. To this day, they are so supportive.

It's funny because I always tell him, "Stop Dad, you have to enjoy life." I would call him the Energizer Bunny—he just keeps going and going! But it's what he loves. I don't think he can retire. He would probably drive himself and my mom crazy.

Dad loves building. He especially loves to build companies. That's what he really enjoys. I never had a negative outlook on how much he worked because he was always home for dinner. During high school when our schedules got busier, we made it into family lunch. So instead of dinner, we would all meet for lunch. I would bring friends home from school, and we would have this big lunch. Even when I worked for my dad, I could just walk into his office and interrupt him. I never felt intimidated. He was always welcoming whenever I walked in, even if he was in a meeting. He would never shoo me out.

My dad always goes the extra mile for people. He is just good. He set a great example for me.

STEVEN BRAILSFORD

Steven is Ken's third son. He is currently involved in property development. He has worked at Zija International and Pharmatech. He, his wife, Amy, and their five children reside in Lehi, Utah.

THE THINGS I PROBABLY ADMIRE MOST about my dad is his honesty and the good example he is to me; also how he provides for his family and creates jobs for people.

As a parent, in terms of discipline, Dad would just show disappointment. That was harder on me than losing privileges or yelling or anything. He never did any of that. I never wanted to disappoint him. He was the kind of dad that you wanted to make him proud. He would say, "Good job, Steve." And I would feel great.

Dad's always been really supportive. He doesn't ever specifically give you direction because I don't think he wants to get in your way. He'll encourage you when you have an idea and say, "Yeah, you should do that," or "You should try that," or "That might be a little hard because of this . . .," but I would never go to my dad and say, "What should I do with my life?" because he'd say, "You've got to figure that out for yourself." He realizes that it's important to find your own vision and dreams.

To see my dad not hide or be ashamed of spiritual things on a professional level has been a major encouragement to me because most business people aren't like that. They don't talk about politics or religion, but Dad realizes that everything he has is from the Lord and he says that to me all the time—that the Lord gave him all this and He can easily take it away.

So that's been a great example to me because I realize that he doesn't put financial success above his children, or above his religion, or above his family. He always puts important things first and everything else seems to follow. It really gives me a good perspective when we're having a successful time financially. We have a better perspective of the importance of not focusing on the next boat or whatever we want to get—that we should focus on family or our beliefs.

Dad has always put the Lord first. This was a great example to me because I wasn't sure I wanted to follow that path. I never questioned Dad's belief. I always knew that *he* knew what he believes is true and he has never wavered. That's been a great example to me. But it was cool because he had a dream that he would go on a mission when he had his last child. So their first mission to Georgia was at the same time I went on my mission to Manchester, England. They got home just as I was getting home. It was wonderful to correspond and share letters about the missions. Dad really wanted to come and serve with me. He wanted to be my last transfer. My mission president would have done it, but it's not the standard, I guess. We both got our mission calls the same day. We went to Elder Ballard's office and opened them up together. It was a neat experience.

I think over the years, Dad has realized that family is what really matters so he's really kind and gentle and loving toward his grandkids. He's always showing affection and is really supportive with them. You can tell he's a really good grandpa. I just admire how Dad's always known what he's supposed to do. It's not an easy thing for everyone to know what they should do in life. But he's always seemed to know what he should do with business and he's done it. He's had the courage to actually do it and succeed.

RYAN PALMER

Ryan is married to Ken's daughter, Becky. Ryan is the President of Zija International.

K EN IS VERY EVEN-KEELED. When you say someone "chews you out," that depicts an image of somebody who has a quick temper and can be angry and unresponsive. But not Ken. He's usually very even-tempered and doesn't have highs and lows. He's pretty consistent and has demonstrated that a leader is someone who is always consistent. You know what to expect, when to expect it, and you know that he will always be there and do what he says he will. You don't have questions about whether or not Ken is going to be available. You *know* that he's going to be available. You *know* that he's going to carry through on his part. You never have to think about it.

So the consistency that he's demonstrated has been one of the leadership attributes that I've learned from Ken. When people are looking to a leader, they are looking to someone they can count on, someone who is adding value. And you can count on the value that Ken is going to add. And it will consistently be there.

I've found over the years working with Ken that he's not an individual who is ever looking at the short-term solution. He's always looking at the big vision, at the back end of what you want to achieve. And he's not willing to make a decision that would mortgage tomorrow for the sake of today.

When Ken made the decision that he was going to invest in and launch Zija International, he called the family together. We met down at the Riverside Country Club in Provo and had dinner. It was at that dinner that Ken told everyone he was coming out of retirement, because at that point in time he *was* retired. It was a pretty significant announcement when he said, "I'm coming out of retirement." However, he also said, "I'm not going to make a commitment to jump back in on a day-to-day basis. I'm going to fund it." And it was in that meeting, that very first meeting, where he said, "This will be my legacy." When Ken talked about legacy, looking at what he had already accomplished with Nature's Sunshine and Enrich International, both companies were tremendously successful. Both are still in business today. So it was a pretty profound statement when he said, "Zija will be my legacy."

He used that dinner meeting as a platform to offer words of wisdom and advice, a real teaching moment for all the children. He talked about the importance of being financially prudent and how to manage finances so that finances don't manage you. And he said when you make a lot of money, don't let your values or your principles change. Don't let the consequence of being financially successful be the downfall of you. Maintain the same principles of integrity, and ethics, and morals that allowed you to arrive at that point. In hindsight, when you look back on it, you can see how Ken had a vision for where this company was going. I got to the point of believing in and trusting Ken and his advice so much, that I would ask myself, when making decisions, "What would Ken do?" and use that as a compass to guide me.

The best piece of advice that Ken has ever given me came in the very first meeting I had with him, and it was advice relative to my marriage and relationship with his daughter, Becky. He told me to prioritize my life based on things of an eternal nature. And that's advice I will certainly heed.

> I believed in and trusted Ken so much that I would ask myself, "What would Ken do?" and I'd use that as my compass.
>
> — RYAN PALMER

What I think would surprise people most about Ken is the fact that there aren't a lot of surprises. He is so consistent in who he is. I think a lot of people would have the same experience that I have in the sense that there's a man behind the persona. And when you get to know that man, you'll find out that he's just as solid as a rock.

I have been gifted with a father-in-law who has been influential in so many different ways—spiritually, personally, emotionally, in business—literally in every facet of my life.

NEAL AND CAROL ADAMS

Neal and Carol are dear friends of Ken and Linda. Other than family, they have been close to Ken and Linda longer than anyone else. Neal is retired from Geneva Steel. They reside in Orem, Utah.

NEAL

I BELIEVE KEN is successful because he really believes in what he's doing. He's able to convince people but he isn't pushy like a lot of people. He's very even-tempered. I've never heard him raise his voice. He's very good at communicating.

After Ken got Nature's Sunshine running, he was traveling so much he decided to get a airplane. So he bought a little Cessna single-engine plane and took his flight lessons. I think the same day he got his solo hours in, he could fly with additional people, so he took Carol and Linda and flew up from the Provo airport to the Salt Lake airport. Then he picked me up at the Provo airport after I got off work at Geneva Steel that afternoon, about 4 or 5 o'clock. So he and I flew from Provo up to Salt Lake to take a cab in and meet our wives and then fly back down.

I'd never been in a small aircraft before. We started out and as we were going north toward Salt Lake, we got to the point of the mountain and started to feel some hard thumps. As we went on, it started getting worse and worse. I said, "This is pretty bumpy," and Ken said, "It's just summertime. It's just hard air, you get it at times around the point when hot air is rising. As soon as we get to the other side, it will level off." We got around the point and I could see out across the Salt Lake valley. There were dust devils everywhere. We must have been flying at about 8,000 or 9,000 feet and those dust devils kept rising up as high as we were almost.

I'll tell you, that little plane started to buck like a bronco and when that altimeter spun down, it felt like the bottom had dropped out. Ken had the radio on, listening to the traffic. You could hear these big airliners warning everyone of turbulence. They were waiting for it to blow over before landing.

Just to the east of the commercial liners was the municipal airport where the Air National Guard and private planes would fly in. They gave Ken a runway to come in on; meanwhile this little plane was dancing and the wind was blowing us toward the mountains so hard, besides us going up and down, that Ken was almost on a 45 degree angle to keep going straight; but all the time he's sitting there just calmly trimming the prop and everything, keeping us right on the track to go in.

He calmly said, "We'll go to this channel," and I said, "Ken, have you ever seen anything like this?" And he said, "Well, no I don't think I've had anything quite this bad." But Ken brought her down and when he got to within several hundred feet of the ground, the air was just as smooth and calm as it could be. And all the time he's just as calm as can be, talking to the guys on the radio, lining himself up, and just tending to business. He was going straight no matter what was going on around us.

A couple years later we were going down to St. George together and I recalled that experience and mentioned it to Ken. He said, "You remember that, too?" I said, "Yeah, if I'd had a parachute, I'd have jumped." And he looked at me and smiled and said, "If we'd had parachutes, we'd have both jumped!" He was just so level-headed and never showed any excitement, just total confidence. He knew what he was doing, and *his* confidence gave me confidence. That's kind of rare in a person.

I admire his consistency. He's the same person I knew thirty-three years ago. We've all changed, we're all seasoned more, but as far as the basic things, charity for people and that, he's still the same. He's never changed. He's the same guy whether he's been sitting on top of the world or the world got turned upside-down. He's the same guy.

CAROL

We met Ken thirty-three years ago. Through my years of friendship with Ken and Linda, I've learned that they really care. Ken cares that the people he works with might have a better life. I believe that's why he's so successful. He has made a better life for many people.

I heard Elder Ballard talk at their first missionary farewell, and he said Ken will teach them the doctrine and Linda will love them into the church. And that just sums how they team up. I think Linda loves everyone so genuinely and so sincerely. And Ken does, too. But he knows his doctrine even better than he knows his business—and he sure knows business!

Linda's definitely the heart of the family. Ken is a wonderful father and both of them would go to the ends of the earth for their kids, but Ken is the business and Linda's the love. And she loves Ken so much. She is such a blessing to everyone who knows her. I feel so blessed and lucky that she is my friend.

I admire Ken's ability to be there and offer help. Whatever people need, he is able to help. That is a blessing and a gift. He's always been a kind and generous person. I know I could call him anytime and he would be there for me. Linda as well. I always say Linda's my sister from another mother. I feel almost the same way about Ken because we just love him to death.

ANN PYNE

Ann has worked for KEB Enterprises and Zija International.

I ACTUALLY MET KEN through my ward in my neighborhood—he was the bishop. Also, my daughter was his secretary. Ken had several small businesses and offered me a job at one of them. I've worked for him for about twenty years now.

> Ken is absolutely the most loyal person I know. If he gives you a handshake, if he says he's going to do something, he will do it.
>
> — ANN PYNE

Dave Shurtliff and I worked at bringing Zija into profitability while Ken was on his mission. Zija was in bad shape, but I really felt strongly that we should not sell. Ken came back from his mission (Mission President of the South Carolina Columbia mission of the LDS Church for three years) and Zija was saved. He's the one that really turned it around.

Ken is absolutely the most loyal person I know. If he gives you a handshake, if he says he's going to do something, he will do it. He does not change the deal and he has the utmost integrity.

He is not afraid of the work or the risks like some people. And he's shown me how to get in there and make things happen. And that's so very critical.

He's funny, too. He might have a white board on the wall and get up in the middle of the night, writing on it, and planning things. He's always thinking about what the next move is going to be on this or that.

Ken has a passion and a gift for what he does. Right now I believe that he feels very responsible for providing jobs in this economy. I think he feels it's a calling because it is something he does well, so he has a responsibility to share that talent with others.

He said one day, "Gee! Yeah, I'm seventy years old, but do I just take what I have and live comfortably on my own, or do I share what I know and what I have with others?"

So I'm a very fortunate woman to have the opportunity to work by his side. I can't say enough. He's supported me and allowed me to keep working even when I had cancer and couldn't work because of all the sick time. He continued to support me. He did not kick me to the curb like so many other employers would. He works hard on doing what's right. And he never gives up on that. It's every single day. It's not just once in a while. It's every single day.

BART ANTHONY

Bart is responsible for property acquisition for KEB Enterprises.

I'M A REAL ESTATE AGENT. I met Ken at an open house one time when he was house hunting. I happened to be showing a home in Orem, back when Ken lived in Cherry Village, right across the street from where this open house was.

We have much more than a real estate relationship now. I consider it a friendship. Ken and I have been working together for over fifteen years.

One of the biggest things I have learned from Ken is that when it comes to transactions, at least real estate transactions, he isn't emotionally attached to the outcome as much as the average person. Ken looks at it as a revenue-generating source, so when he looks at a piece of real estate, he looks at its return or its utility value, but definitely not the emotional aspect of "I'm emotionally invested in this, therefore I cannot walk away from it." I think that's one of the reasons that Ken is successful because he doesn't dwell on opportunities that he's missed because he's already on his way to new opportunities. Sometimes when we miss an opportunity, we lament over it for so long that it consumes our time and slows down our ability to be productive. No so with Ken.

> Ken does know numbers, and he has a memory like an elephant. He takes his grandkids to the zoo, and the only animals that will go in their hut and not come out are the elephants, because they are intimidated by Ken's memory!
>
> — BART ANTHONY

One thing that surprised me, and it would make me laugh and cry, is that I consider Ken a "deposit junkie." It doesn't matter how much the deposit is, but if an amount can be deposited into his account, it makes him happy. Just like a peanut butter shake makes me happy, a deposit makes Ken happy. When Ken hired me to be his exclusive real estate agent, we started a company called Castlerock Real Estate.

When I worked with Ken in the KEB offices in Riverwoods on the third floor, I was working for him exclusively. When he wasn't keeping me busy, I would be doing just simple residential real estate and would split that commission with Ken because I was on his payroll. So that made sense.

Take a $110,000 lot where I'd make 3% of the commission. Divide that in half. Then take someone of Ken's caliber who has people vying for his time and attention since he has money everywhere (you know that there are people doing much more lucrative deals than Bart Anthony of Castlerock Real Estate). But if I closed on a lot and there was a deposit coming in, by the time you split it down, $1200 would go into KEB's account and $1200 into mine. Ken would ask me about that deposit two or three times a day until the deposit got into his account. And I just used to smile about that because I would walk away and he would say, "Did we get that deposit yet?" I'd think, "I know you've got four other appointments today that by far trump my $1200 commission deposit that's going into KEB's account." But he does not forget! Once again, it really shows the reason I believe Ken is financially successful—he watches his dollars.

I think people would be surprised to know how down

to earth Ken really is. I just smile sometimes when I have to meet him somewhere and he's in Levis and a flannel shirt. Even if he were wearing a Rolex watch, he 'd carry himself in such a way that you would never look to see if he had a Rolex; but I would almost bet you a peanut butter shake that he doesn't have a Rolex watch, unless somebody bought it for him as a gift. He is so unpretentious.

I think people would be surprised at how approachable Ken is and how much he really does care. And I think they would be surprised that he really does have a humorous side.

Ken doesn't show his emotions on his sleeve like some people. I think he is humble, quiet, and keen at allowing people to keep their dignity. This is one talent, or piece of wisdom, that Ken keeps key people in the company in order to allow the company to be successful. Like with Lehi Roller Mills, why go and reinvent the wheel and have someone come back in and learn wheat when you have a four-generation wheat expert?

Ken also has the kind of brain that just won't shut off. He continues to work. He could have retired when he sold Enrich, but he didn't. He could have said, "I've paid my dues. I'm going to retire." But one of Ken's core characteristic traits is he is a hard worker, and when you have that habit from the beginning, you can't turn it off in your fifties or sixties. He's up early. He calls late.

I think because Ken's so successful, the average person who crosses paths with him might become intimidated by his success and wealth. But he's just a compassionate person, an ordinary person who has become quietly extraordinary.

DAVID SHURTLIFF

Dave is Ken's cousin. He has worked at Enrich International, Zija International, and KEB Enterprises. He has been one of Ken's best friends and trusted advisors. He resides in Draper, Utah with his wife.

Ken and I grew up very close to each other. I would go as far as to say we are more like brothers than cousins. We have a large family and there are lot of cousins, but Ken was like the big brother I always wanted. He has always looked out for me and wanted to make sure I was included. When we were together, he would take me along to whatever he was doing.

Ken was always glad to serve in church. I would visit him and was so proud of him. One of my memories was when Ken became a deacon. He was passing the sacrament. I was about four or five years old. Another deacon brought the sacrament to me and I said, "No thanks, I'm waiting for Ken to bring me mine."

Ken's parents were just fabulous people. Ken got the best of each of them. My mother's favorite story of Ken—and if I could tell only one story it would be this one because this is what my mother told me on her death bed—was when she was ten days away from the end of her life. When I was little and Ken was in his early teens, he would tell me Bible stories at night. My mother used to sneak down the hallway to listen. Ken loved the gospel and was always sharing it along with his testimony.

As a child, he was my big brother, the kind that you want to be like. I think he inspired that in a lot of people. It's very infectious because he's very genuine, very honest, sincere, and open. He's not somebody that goes to church because he wants to be seen at church, or reads a particular book because he wants to be seen reading that book. You recognize immediately that Ken's the real deal

He has so much of the light of Christ. Imagine a networking CEO where you really have to be a crowd pleaser and have to inspire people. Ken gets up on stage and talks about religion and his relationship with our Savior. He does that in front of thousands of people with no regard as to what they're religious beliefs might be. He doesn't preach Mormonism, although he makes it clear what his religion is. But he shares his feelings of Christ. He does what his Savior would have him do.

> Ken is best example I know of someone who is blessed because of his character, because of his love for our Heavenly Father.
> — DAVID SHURTLIFF

Ken is the best example I know of someone who is blessed because of his character, because of his love for our Heavenly Father. When Ken was Mission President, we may have saved the company from dying, but we did not do well with the company. We were close to flat-lining and tried lots of things. I believe that this company was waiting for Ken to come back. It was his right and privilege to take the company forward. And there had come a time that there was nothing I could have done. Heavenly Father was waiting for Ken to come back.

To Ken, it's all about people. It's not just about products. There are huge successful marketing companies that sell widgets. It doesn't matter what they sell, it's about the compensation plan. Network marketing has a bad rep because for some things, if you don't have a good product, it's a scheme. But if you have legitimate product, you have a distribution channel. Everyone doesn't succeed at it; but we have products in every company that Ken has been involved in, so if no one ever made a dime, the products were still beneficial. Ken has seen to that. Ken wouldn't sell widgets.

BRENT ASHWORTH

Brent is Ken's cousin. He is an attorney and rare documents and antiquities collector. He has worked at both Nature's Sunshine Products and Zija International. He resides in Provo, Utah.

I'M KEN'S FIRST COUSIN. His father, Bob, and my mother were brother and sister. I'm just a little younger than him. I remember we used to visit our grandparents who lived in Provo. We would get together as kids and he would try to teach us how to play Monopoly. I've laughed about that because I've asked his kids, "Well, has your dad ever played Monopoly with you?" And they'd say, "Yeah, he always beats us." And I would say, "That's the way it was with us, too. He always positioned himself as the banker. Well, by the time I tried to teach my kids how to play Monopoly, they were calling me a cheater because I had all these additional rules I learned from Ken.

Most people don't look at the fine print and the rules in Monopoly, but they are little things involving interest and details like that. I mean it was really more real life with Ken. I figured early on that he probably had this thing for money because he had a good head on his shoulders when it came to that. He didn't let the rules of a game keep him from making it more interesting and exciting. It could be a fairly long-lasting game and he made it very interesting by so many innovations that he made to it. I enjoyed playing with him. It was a lot of fun. You could never beat him but that didn't seem to bother any of us. I've always loved Ken. He's a great guy.

I always remember Ken's dad being very serious. Ken's mother, Freeda, was also a very bright lady and very concerned about others. It was when my mother was dying of cancer that Freeda didn't just give up like the rest of the family. She came up with these herbal remedies and things like that to help her. So Ken grew up with an appreciation of that early on. Both his parents were very sweet people and they were both very unique. You know Bob brought the brains as far as he was a scientist. He was methodical in his thinking and I think he passed a lot of that along to Ken. Ken is very meticulous; he thinks through things pretty clearly before he jumps into something. And he can do it quite quickly. Ken's been a real support over the years.

I went through school at BYU and Ken and I actually took a beginning economics class together. It was the only class I had with him. We've always been very close; he's kind of been the big brother I didn't have and he sort of took me under his wing. We share a lot of family history.

I admire the fact that Ken sets goals quite a few people will say are out of reach but he reaches them. And he sets

> Ken is a modern-day Tom Sawyer!
>
> — BRENT ASHWORTH

big goals! Ken is a modern-day Tom Sawyer. He can get anyone else in town to paint the fence. Ken does a lot of the work, too. I'm not trying to imply that he isn't a hard worker. But he has a natural ability to influence others—I think this is one of the reasons that he succeeds. He also has a vision of the end goal in mind. A lot of people don't have that, Most of us are kind of like blue bottle flies. A blue bottle fly is a fly that you could put in a mason jar and take the lid off and they would stay in the jar even though they could be free. Ken is one of those that would fly out. He'd know that the lid was gone.

One way he does this is he has high expectations of his employees and the people that work with him. He expects them to be able to accomplish what he sets out for them to do, and it's not that he is trying to make things impossible. Sometimes they can meet the goal; sometimes they can't. He sets the bar really high and then he has a lot of faith in people. He gives them the ability to move. He may know the answers, but he likes to give people enough rope. I don't think he thinks that any of us are going to fail and he gives us the freedom and resources to make decisions to meet our goals.

I think if people were to follow Ken for a day, if they were observant, they would learn a lot. Ken is so natural at it and it comes to him so easily that people may underestimate him until they actually are able to see what he is able to accomplish. He is a real, nice, humble guy. You don't get the impression that he is going to overlord you like some bosses do. He figures out what your abilities are and then he treats you well and seems to have a lot of faith in you. He believes you can accomplish those things.

He is very unique. I remember going with him when he first picked up Lehi Roller Mills. I was recently at Alpine Air with him and followed him around from office to office. Here he is, the big boss, but he allows them to do their jobs. Not only that, he lets them know he has faith in them, and I truly think he believes they can do the job, which makes them want to jump to the level to which he is asking them to perform.

I have observed something in Ken over the years. He is just as bold as he ever was, but now he's a lot brighter. I worked with him at Nature's Sunshine Products as legal counsel in the beginning days. Then I was his attorney at Zija for a couple of years. He went on a mission and then he had me back a couple years ago. I noticed that he has gotten a lot wiser. Even if he didn't like what you were saying, he showed a lot of respect for what you were trying to do.

One lesson to be learned from Ken is how to work with people and how to get people to work with you. He can move people because he figures them out. He allows people to be their best, which I think is why he is so successful. I don't always agree with him and he doesn't always agree with me but we always respect each other and love each other, and I think as a result of that, we have always been able to work together. He knows that I'm always trying to protect his backside and I know he is always there for me.

RAY AND BEVERLY DEGOOYER

Ray is Ken's brother-in-law. He owned and operated his own commercial real estate appraisal firm in Green River, Wyoming. Currently he has different entrepreneurial ventures that he's involved in. Beverly is Linda's sister, and Ray is her husband. Beverly is a homemaker. They reside in St. George, Utah.

RAY

K EN'S BEEN A GREAT BROTHER-IN-LAW and a good example to the rest of the family. He's certainly shown what good, hard work can do and how to keep your focus on where your goals are.

I think he's stretched out to help different family members when they're in need of advice. I've watched how he's schooled his kids, particularly in their later years. I've watched him give advice and counsel them to do the right thing and make the right decisions.

He's got a good intellect and he's honest in what he does. He's been through a lot of trials. He's shown he can come through them and still have his integrity and stay positive. So these are a few of his strong character traits.

Ken has a variety of businesses. He has to make decisions that aren't popular sometimes, yet he can be very compassionate. From that aspect, most people may not consider him to be compassionate when he really is.

We as a family are proud of him and of the example that he's setting for others to follow. I've loved the way he's loved and taken care of Linda.

BEVERLY

I WAS ACQUAINTED WITH KEN in high school in Bakersfield, California but didn't really have a conversation with him. We didn't grow up together while going to school. I remember him being quiet but personable. We were in the same church stake and I would sometimes see him at church activities. I was already married and living in Utah by the time he started dating Linda. I remembered who he was, though, and that he was a nice young man.

When Ken and Linda were first married, Ray (my husband) and I, and our other sister, Glenna, and Denny (her husband) would get together. We'd eat and play games. Ken loves to play games! He wasn't used to being social and sometimes he'd just want to read his book. But if it was a game he was interested in, and he was very competitive, he'd play.

We had fun vacations, too. We went to Hawaii. And when you are on vacation with Ken, he's "go, go, go" and wants to see everything. He'd come home every night exhausted from how busy the day was.

Ken has worked very hard. And I'm not surprised at all at his success. One of the things that I admire about him is his drive and his motivation and the fact that growing up as an only child, he was mature beyond his years. "Only" children seem to mature earlier because they're more often around adults growing up.

I admire Ken's strong faith and his incredible work ethic. Plus he's just a very loving, kind, giving person, very generous, and has always been there for our family. I consider him a brother.

KEVIN DEGOOYER

Kevin is Ken's nephew. He works as Purchasing and Logistics Manager at Pharmatech.

KEN HAS SOME GREAT QUALITIES as far as people skills and knowing how to interact with others. He makes people feel comfortable and that they're being heard. And he has great leadership qualities. He instills his vision within them and helps them to see the whole picture and succeed. He gives people opportunities to ask questions and learn from all of his experience. His knowledge from working in such different industries has helped him succeed.

I believe his success comes from his drive, his dedication, his thirst for knowledge. When he learns something, he wants to know more; he dives into it fully, gets more information. He has been able to look at the risks involved and take that chance. He surrounds himself with good people who can help manage some of the things going on so he doesn't have to see to every detail. But he is always in the know. He has his finger on the pulse all the time.

He comes and sits down in my office sometimes and he'll ask, "How are you doing?" And my standard answer is, "You know, I'm doing good." But he'll stop me for a second and say, "No, *how are you doing?*" So he wants to get to know how I'm doing on a personal level, not just a business level.

Ken has done that with other people, not just family. I've seen him stop and talk with a worker in the warehouse or one of the production crew and he gets to know them. He'll ask them about their lives, and he remembers it so the next time he sees them he'll say, "Oh, how was this and this?" or "What's going on in your life?" And they'll say, "Well, yeah, it's turned around. And it's great." And they come out feeling happy. It makes me happy to see that he's spreading that to others as well as to me.

I appreciate that Ken gives me opportunities to progress in the business. It's one of these family things. You kind of think is he giving you the hand-up because you're family and trying to help you progress, but I'd gone through a regular interview with Ken, and he said, "You know, it's up to somebody else. I'm giving you the interview, but it's up to you to get the job and do it."

But he gave me that opportunity. Then he saw the other aspects that I was capable of so I had the opportunity at Pharmatech. He encouraged me and said, "Hey, would you like to go to this other company that we have and be able to do that?" And I made it successful down there. He's given me the tools to be able to succeed.

DENNY AND GLENNA SMITH

Denny and Glenna are Ken's brother-in-law and sister-in-law. Denny worked at Enrich International as General Manager of Russia. Denny does marketing and sales for Wisdom Teeth Only, and Glenna is a homemaker. They reside in Pleasant Grove, Utah.

DENNY

I MET KEN in August of 1967. Other than Glenna, I have known Ken longer than most people on earth and have seen him in many circumstances because we're related. One thing about Ken I noticed over the years is his quiet confidence. A lot of people, when they think of "confidence," sometimes they're thinking "overbearing," or "loud," or "boisterous," or even "demanding." Ken is a very Type A personality, but it's a quiet type. In all the years I've known him, I've never seen him really mad. The thing that upsets him the most is when people disappoint him. Usually, it's if someone's cheated him.

With Ken I've learned you've just got to take advantage of the opportunities that present themselves when they do. He's is usually first on the airplane. And he's the first one off. He doesn't waste time. He's very organized in his mind. Yet, I've never seen him really hurt anyone's feelings, even though I've seen people cheat him and deceive him. He'll get upset and say, "Gosh darn it!" or "What the heck?" He doesn't swear. He's not vulgar. He's not vile. He's a man of integrity. Everything he's ever told me that he would do for me, he has done. He has done things for my family and for me personally that no one knows about. And I happen to know he's done a lot for others that others don't know about. He has helped many people behind the scenes. And that's the way it should be.

Of all the people I've ever met in my life, Ken has more integrity, is more brutally honest, and has blessed my life more than any other individual I can think of. I live in a beautiful home, I drive nice cars, I have a good life because of my association with Ken Brailsford. I think, if you ask around, a lot of people are in that same situation. Their association with Ken directly or indirectly has really improved their lives both financially, spiritually, and socially.

I've had an opportunity to travel with Ken. I have seen the world. I've had an opportunity to get to know his friends and family. I have great respect for Ken Brailsford. He has been true blue to Linda since day one, and to his family. He's a devoted family man. You can't talk about Ken without talking about Linda. Linda and Ken. I can't imagine them without each other. They're just two peas in a pod, just like a marriage should be. So what I have learned from Ken and Linda is devotion to spouse, devotion to working hard to succeed, and being motivated to bless the lives of others. He's done that his whole life.

GLENNA

W HEN I FIRST KNEW KEN, he had just started dating Linda. I thought he was pretty boring because he was quiet. He didn't talk much. He was reserved. I knew he was very smart. I just felt uncomfortable around him until I got to know him better. We all started doing things together, then I realized that he had a fun side to him.

What I appreciate about Ken is he's just matter of fact. He tells it like it is. He doesn't pussyfoot around with things that he needs to say. He makes you stop and think about things, too. He has a way of doing that. Ken has taught me that when you need to get going, you go, and before you judge, listen. I've never seen him misjudge people.

SHERMAN ROBINSON

Sherman is the grandson of George Robinson, founder of Lehi Roller Mills, where he runs the day-to-day operations.

FOR A FEW YEARS, Ken knew he was going to be involved in some way with Lehi Roller Mills, but he just didn't know how. He stepped in when we needed some serious help. As he grew to learn more, he was very supportive. When we needed more capital, I went to Kyle (with KEB) and answers from Ken came through him. Then eventually Ken and I started communicating, just between the two of us, and that's how it's going now.

Ken comes in and talks with everyone, then meets with me directly. We have more than quadrupled sales so far this year. We're in close to 3,000 stores across the United States right now. I always felt that Ken deserved the utmost respect for what he did in supplying the financial backing for the mill. I still respect it. I think what's grown between us is a realization that what he has brought to the mill has allowed all the employees to stay there.

What keeps me coming into work is that twenty-five people are employed here and their families depend on us. Also the mill plays an important role in agriculture in the area and the fabric of the community. Ken has said that he always felt he would be involved with Lehi Roller Mills someday. I know that he made a sacrifice to buy the mill, and I know that he did it partly to save jobs. I had other opportunities to go work elsewhere, but I stayed because I know that I have in me what the mill needs to succeed.

I can't begin to express what it means to me that Ken saved these jobs here. Lehi Roller Mills would not be where it is today without Ken and without my input. It's absolutely remarkable what the mill's done. There isn't a day that goes by that if I meet someone that finds out that I work at Lehi Roller Mills that they don't say that they're so glad it's still here and that it's important. My milling heritage can be traced back to England in the 1600's, then Delaware in 1700's and in Utah in the 1800's. I have flour in my veins and Ken is probably on his way to having it in his veins as well.

CATHY YEATES

Cathy works as the VP of New Market Development for Zija International.

I STARTED WITH ZIJA International IN 2006. It's been the last five years that I've worked closely with Ken. I was told that everyone in this industry has worked with Ken at one point or another and that he is a no-nonsense guy. He has been called the "father of herbal encapsulation." But most importantly, he is known as a man of integrity. I was with another network marketing company but jumped ship to come to Zija because of Ken's reputation. I love working for no-nonsense people and I want stability and integrity.

Ken has always been steady and encouraging and making sure I understood what set of problems I would probably encounter. He's amazing; he's sees the whole picture. He always tells me I have work integrity and a great work ethic. *He* has an amazing work ethic. I try to be the leader that people respect and I use him as my example; he walks the walk. He doesn't have to—that man is in the office almost every day. It's not because he wants to micromanage you; it's not because he wants to be that big guy; it's because he wants to see this company be successful, and *he wants to see you be successful.* At the core of Ken is a strong work ethic, integrity, for sure, and tenacity.

Ken is very much family-driven with his immediate family. What I love about it is he holds them to a higher level than others. But I think he's a fair guy. He sees it like it is and he tells it like it is. One way to describe him would be "high impact leadership."

And Ken has an amazing woman backing him. Linda is just a doll and I see her with her family and hear them talking about her. I mean, behind every great man is a great woman. I'm sure Ken would not be where he is without Linda. If I had a living father, I would want him to be like Ken. He has the kind of integrity I would want to see in my father. He's brought out the best in me and encouraged me. He sees my potential. That's why I'm here and I don't want to let him down.

JOE FORD

Joe is the Operation Manager at Elements of Healthcare.

ABOUT TWO YEARS AGO, Rodney Larsen, who was then the CEO at Zija and a good friend of mine I'd worked with in the past, knew that I was looking for a new position and said, "You should come over and talk to Ken. We've got something going that might be just perfect for you."

So I went over to the Zija office, since I lived close by, and had a great conversation with him—we have a lot of things in common. We both went through the Army, we both did their OCS program, we both served as platoon leaders and company officers, so we had some things to talk about; and it was kind of fun. He explained what he had in mind for me to do. It sounded great, very flexible, and *it sounded good*. We visited for a long time, more than an hour, more than you would expect for a first interview. What a nice guy!

> Ken doesn't live in the twilight, and he knows mainly victory, because he does make decisions and move forward.
>
> — JOE FORD

I went home and it couldn't have been more than ten minutes when my phone rang. It was Ken. He said, "Can you come back?" I went back and he said, "I want to offer you the position."

I'm a real believer in taking action. Any success that any person has is because they took an action. I'm a firm believer in that and Ken really exemplifies it—you have to take action, you have to do something. He'll make decisions and then he's off. It's fun to see him in action.

Ken's got great character and a strong personality, but he's quiet and soft-spoken, and that's an interesting combination. I see that in his decision-making process. He delegates a lot of things to people, especially in the negotiation process. He doesn't necessarily get involved, so I'll go to him and explain the situation and he'll say, "These are the things that I want to do next or have happen next." That's the kind of situation where you want him to be in control, but you also want to be allowed to do what you do best. It's a great lesson to learn. Surround yourself with good, competent people and use their talents and abilities to make the most progress, have the most success.

I appreciate Ken's soft-spoken manner probably because sometimes I'm a little too loud and a little too noisy. Maybe that's okay but sometimes a whisper is the loudest thing you should say, and I've noticed that about him.

Ken's a great guy to work for, and truthfully, I've never felt like I've worked for him—I feel like I work *with* him. He always treats me more like a peer than an employee, so I always feel like I'm working with him as opposed to working for him. And I feel like I'm his friend. He's always friendly and never patronizing.

KAYLYNE NEWELL

KayLyne is Ken's niece, the daughter of Denny and Glenna Smith. She currently works for the Governor's office in Olympia, Washington. Previously she worked at Enrich International. She and her husband, Matt, reside in Tacoma, Washington.

I N THE EARLY DAYS OF ENRICH, I remember my uncle Ken walking around at the end of every day. He would count how many applications had been faxed in and how many had been processed because we were doing data entry nonstop, getting all the distributors switched over to Enrich. So he would just continually count how many applications. And I thought at the time, "Okay, he's counting." Now I realize that that's actually great leadership strength because he was applying that Biblical principle of knowing the status of your flock.

> Ken's core values never waver. He never compromises those.
>
> — KAYLYNE NEWELL

Looking back, I can see Ken was always thinking about work. Yet he was present with us, too. He was always engaged. I have fond memories of having Thanksgiving dinner or a barbecue outside. He had a good balance between work and family. He didn't often yell, but when he did, there was a reason for it.

I'm amazed ar Ken's "Midas Touch." I admire him as a person. He's a visionary. And he knows when it's time to stay in and when it's time to get out. He has a really good read on the pulse and the timing of things. He doesn't get stars in his eyes. He doesn't say, "This is it. This is going to be the end all to end all." He's constantly looking to diversify and I just admire that he isn't afraid to delve into new areas.

Ken has owned convenience stores, ostrich farms, airlines, he has an interest in a home manufacturing business, Lehi Roller Mills, and more. He's not afraid. He's always looking for great opportunities and he genuinely enjoys transforming a company from failure to success. You have to be really thick-skinned to do what Ken does. You have to be tenacious. And you have to have a clear vision and know how to communicate that to get people to transform with you. He has changed management principles off the charts. And he knows how to align himself with good people. Good leaders. He knows how to bring up good leaders to help him with his vision. And he's a humble enough guy to say, "I don't do it alone." Ken's core values never waver. He never compromises those.

DARIN SMITH

Darin is Ken's nephew. He currently works for Alpine Air. He resides in Orem, Utah with his wife, Pamela.

IT'S FUN WORKING WITH KEN—he's a really good guy who cares about everybody, and he's fun because he has a great sense of humor. I knew he had a sense of humor and he really opened up once I got to know him more. One funny story I remember is he told us when he was a kid, he would play Monopoly by himself. One day his mom came in the room saying it was dinner time and he was upset because he hadn't finished the game!

Ken has helped me professionally—there were times when I would express my experience in my past work—like when I worked at a truck shop—and he reminded me that I don't fit in with the rowdy crowd, that if I worked with him, he would make sure I would be treated fairly.

This is funny . . . but Ken taught me to eat faster—we'd be at lunch and I would take two or three bites and he would be out the door, so I would have to hurry and eat.

I admire Ken's charisma, his knowledge and wisdom. He's always given me good advice when I've asked him for it.

Ken's a very private person. He doesn't tell you everything he's doing. So I was surprised by how many companies he owns. There are some companies I've never even heard about. And he has this aura. He gives pep talks. He doesn't beat around the bush and just tells it like it is.

BRYAN AND KELLY HUGHES

Bryan is Linda's brother. He is retired from OCI Chemicals and resides in Green River, Wyoming, with his wife, Kelly, a homemaker.

BRYAN

I WAS THIRTEEN YEARS OLD when I first met Ken. I thought he was very nice and polite and kind to my mom and dad. Linda started dating him, which was kind of a surprise because she was writing a missionary at the time!

There are several qualities in Ken that I admire. One is hard work. The other is honesty. And he treats people fairly.

I lived with Ken and Linda one summer when they were in the Army at Ft. Bragg in North Carolina. I was fourteen years old. To this day I don't know what he was working on. Some Top Secret thing. I just remember him telling us that he was working on Top Secret stuff. To get into the building they were in, he would push the air conditioner in and crawl through the opening from outside. I just remember it was kind of fun living on the base.

Kenny was just little then and I had fun being an uncle. Linda let me go on my first date. She drove us to a theater. I was only fourteen—and I never told my mom.

I remember when they were living in Springville and their kids were young. Kenny and John were arguing about something. Ken told them to quit arguing and they wouldn't. So he just stopped the car and said, "You can just walk home." And he made them walk home! It was only up the hill, though. But I don't think they ever argued in the car again.

He started his business in a small garage in Orem. It's amazing to see how far he's come. He's been so good to me— letting me stay at the condos at Park City with all my doctors and procedures I've had to have done this last year. I've always offered to pay rent, and he won't take it. He's always, always generous.

KELLY

I met Ken when I was engaged to Bryan. It was the first time that I met the Hughes family in Utah. I stayed with Ken and Linda in their home, and Bryan stayed with Robert and Betty in their home. So I was there with them and their young children by myself. They made me feel like I was part of their family and I'd never felt so comfortable. I felt like their home was my home. The thing that intrigued me so much was I was so impressed with Ken's love of books because I love books, too. They had a little reading loft in their home, so Ken and I hit it off really well because of that shared love of books. We're both only children so we have a bond that way in the large Hughes family. It's kind of a different experience when you marry into a large family when you're an only child. We understand each other—that we need alone time, time to ourselves once in awhile.

If you met Ken on the street, you wouldn't know the kind of man he is—generous and thoughtful. He will do anything he can to make you comfortable, to make things right for you. He tries hard to see that everyone is able to have a good quality of life, to have everything that they could possibly need, many times without them knowing that he did it for them. In essence, Ken goes to people's rescue. He just seems to be that kind of a person. He rescues them but doesn't make them dependent upon him. I think that Ken helps people learn how to take care of themselves, but he also knows how to help them and then send them on their way feeling good about themselves.

Ken is one of the most compassionate and understanding people, yet he has high expectations of everyone. He wants people to succeed. He sets high goals for everyone and expects them to meet his expectations. He is honest in everything he does and has high integrity. I think this is the greatest characteristic that he has.

My favorite memory with Ken is from a few years ago. All of Linda's siblings and spouses, us included, went to South Dakota together and had a wonderful time. We were all in Ken's big van. We were just like a bunch of teenagers driving through Wyoming, South Dakota, and Montana. The most fun we had was when we went shopping at gift shops and debated whether we should try to pan for gold.

Ken is really family-oriented. There's a sparkle in his eye when he looks at Linda and there's nothing he loves more in this world than her.

JAROM DASTRUP

Jarom is VP of Sales for the Americas and Europe for Zija International.

I'LL NEVER FORGET my first experience with Ken. He came walking through Zija with his daughter, Sheri. I was standing outside of Ryan's office, so Sheri introduced me to Ken. We had met casually before, but this was the first official meeting. I had been with Zija for three months at that point. And Sheri was kind. I'd lost my father in a tragic plane crash which she mentioned to Ken. Ken's son, Kenny, came up in that conversation. So we kind of had that commonality that we were able to build from.

Ken looked at me square in the eyes and said, "Jarom, I want to give you a project." And I'll be honest, I was trembling because I didn't know him. I hadn't had a relationship with him. And this man that I'd heard so much about and I'd spent hours on the phone telling people about, was looking me in the face saying, "Here's a project." And the project was autoship retention.

He said, "We don't have any type of metrics or account-ability or anything to help with autoship retention. So I'm empowering you to go do that. Go make it happen and send me a weekly report on how the company is doing." It was a huge task because I was still in the learning process. I wasn't familiar with what all of the back office software could do. So for a couple of months there, I manually did that report for Ken every week.

When Ken knows that something needs to be done, he will empower the individual and give them complete confidence and trust that they will get it done. If they don't get it done, then there's a consequence. But if they do get it done, he will empower them again and again. And he actually took everything I said and implemented it. I felt valued. And I felt that I was contributing to this man's legacy, that I was adding value to what he believes—what this whole mission in life is. And the influence that he has, and the fact that he was taking what I had to say and implementing it, well, my sense of value was through the roof! It was a great experience. It was awesome!

Ken's leadership style is very empowering. And by the same token, the minute you take advantage of that, he's very quick to pull that from you. One thing that I have learned about Ken is he is about second chances as long as he believes the person is being honest with him. I've literally seen that happen.

I would say the things I've learned most from Ken are these: when you have a conviction of whatever it is that you're doing, working on, or believing in, don't ever forget that conviction. I can only imagine there have been times when Ken has said, "Am I throwing good money after bad?" Because of the conviction that he had before and the belief that he was doing was right, he stayed the course and relied on that conviction.

The next thing I've learned is loyalty. In some of the scenarios that I've shared, I've seen him make what I call an "acting" contract, or a "hand-shake" contract. His word is as good as putting it in a binding contract. If he tells you that he's going to do something, then he will absolutely deliver, as long as you keep up your end of the bargain. There's one scenario that I can think of where it cost him hundreds of thousands of dollars. And it was an honest mistake that was made. But because of the loyalty of the people that it affected, Ken fulfilled the obligation even though it cost him hundreds of thousands of dollars. And I witnessed that first hand.

I've also learned that regardless of who you believe your Creator is, to never be ashamed of it. That doesn't necessarily mean that you have to be preaching it and always talking about it. But it's actions. It's, "What are you doing? Does your heart line up with your actions and do your actions line up with your words?" I've seen him speak about these principles and about his Creator and his belief and his personal relationship without even saying that is what it is. And I've implemented that in my own life.

KEN BRAILSFORD

179

MARK LISONBEE

Mark is a long time friend and former employee of Ken's.

I WORKED WITH KEN off and on through the years, and at one point, I received a job offer for somewhere else. I was nervous, but he was supportive. That really made me feel confident in going on to the next job. I knew that Ken had left the door open to keep our relationship so I could have an opportunity to work with him again.

We were in the same ward together for a long time in Orem, so I knew Ken through church. We've had a relationship for years, one of mutual respect for each other. And we knew how each other worked. About a year and a half ago, we started doing deals together. It was just like nothing had stopped. It had been about twenty-five years since we'd worked full time together, maybe thirty years. It was almost like a homecoming for me. I really enjoyed that experience to be able to sit down with Ken again. I know how he thinks. I know what he likes. And I'm able to work on deals with him again.

In my experience with Ken, if there's a disagreement about something, we can sit down and he's not so arrogant or bull-headed that we can't compromise. I think that's something that's grown over the years. I notice it in Ken more and I think it has a lot to do with his success—the fact that he's willing to take input, analyze that, and, set all ego aside and do his best for the company or for a particular person.

I admire Ken's ability to get into the details of the business and make tough decisions. There's nothing harder in business than to come in, take a company that's not doing well, that's losing money, and turn it around. It's the most difficult thing. A start up (starting fresh with a brand new company) is much easier. Starting with a company that's profitable is much easier. To change the whole dynamic of a company, the whole way a company is run, and start fresh that way and turn it around when it's already going down the road the wrong way, is the most difficult.

Our relationship has been really rewarding. It's like ten percent is the business, so we get that out of the way. Here's A, B, C, or D. We'll get that done. And then we'll spend eighty, ninety percent of the time talking about what's happening in the world or religion.

DR. JOSHUA PLANT

Josh is the VP of Research and Development at Zija International.

THE FIRST TIME I MET KEN was at the temple where he was a sealer. I was brought in for research and development at Zija and the first time I met him professionally, we talked. He's a person who is very intrigued with the small steps along with the big picture. He was shooting around ideas and there was a lot of innovative dialogue.

I would say I work *with* Ken versus working *for* him. He's my elder, but you wouldn't know it by the way he works. His physical energy is better than that of a twenty-year-old. He's also got a very open door. I'll go and share an idea with him and his door is always open. Even in the middle of the night,

I can get hold of him. He's very encouraging to others. He doesn't lose contact with people and finds time for everyone.

When I have an idea, Ken looks at it from all angles and makes sure that it can benefit the company. He's got a very sharp mind. But he also has a lot of longevity. I lean on that extensively. Working in business is measuring risk, essentially. His ability to do that is through his experience. I've relied on his experience. We all have to anchor ourselves on Ken's experience and the likeliness of him not succeeding is slim. There's no formal training for it. I'm just as trained as the guy walking down the street, but we need Ken, and that's the reason that all of these businesses have succeeded.

Ken is interesting; he has a unique sense of humor and it comes out when you least expect it. He's able to bring in humor to help the business get done. His humor is sparse and random. Sometimes he breaks tension with a joke and uses humor as a way of allowing people to relax and not be so tense. He likes to tease his kids.

The most surprising thing about Ken is the lack of surprise. He's just as religious when he's talking to an Apostle as he is talking to thousands of distributors. He's the same Ken no matter what situation or environment he's in. He's not a chameleon. His environment is a product of him, not the other way around. When you get into the business world, you realize that integrity sometimes gets shoved to the side. People are compromising every value they represent for a dollar. What's reassuring about Ken is I don't have to be like that to be successful. It's something that I've tried to remember, doing what's right will always bless you.

Ken has exceptional leadership skills, but he is also a good follower. When he's around Linda, you realize who the CEO is. He does it out of reverence and love toward her. He invited me to dinner once and brought the food to Linda. He asked what she wanted and was a servant to her. You can be a powerful leader, but you don't have to be a dictator. He has shown that in professional relationships and family relationships.

SCOTT ROBERTS

Scott is currently the CEO for Pharmatech.

KEN KNOWS WHAT HE'S DOING. When I was interviewing with him and discussing salary he said, "If you're here in six months, I'll pay you what you're asking for." It told me immediately that Ken is no-nonsense. What he says will happen, will happen. "I have every confidence that you will be here in six months," is what he said to me. He will make things right and lives by his word. He's a good guy to work for. By the way, I've been here longer than six months.

At the end of the day Ken trusts his people, which is huge. I've worked for people where it feels like you're constantly being micromanaged. He has enough going on and lets people do what they do best. You want to be able to spread your wings and that's possible with Ken. I've made decisions that I have thought were best for the company and he has allowed me to do that and backs me up. Ken will come in, you're working, and bam! He's there. Two seconds later, he's gone.

In general, he puts it on you to go through the process and supports you. He's not trying to do everything. He couldn't be where he's at if he did. In the end, he's very savvy and smart. But watch out because he's going to call your bluff if you don't know what you're talking about. If he gets information he's questioning, he'll make sure it's correct or not.

Something that I see in Ken I've seen in some other people to an extent. I'm all about managing finances and the value of a dollar. Every dollar matters to Ken. He respects the value of money and spends it wisely. Rich people make good decisions. That is generally why they're rich. Ken values his employees, but he will pay what is fair. Some will want more, but he's smart with his money.

I feel like Ken trusts me. He has me here as the lead guy. What little interaction there has been is evidence that he trusts me. What more could you want than that? He's allowing me to grow and develop. He must see something in me. He's put people in place and allows us to do our jobs.

BEN MEAD

Ben is the President and CEO of GeoPower. He and his family reside in Manila, Philippines.

KEN AND I WORK TOGETHER CLOSELY. We've built a great business relationship. I was introduced to Ken by a mutual contact, Mark Lisonbee. I founded GeoPower in Australia and had an opportunity to develop a large bio-gas project in Utah. It's actually the world's largest generator of renewable power that uses methane captured from pig waste. I relocated the head office to Utah and started developing that project, as well as a range of other projects, from the Park City head office. I was seeking a relationship with an investor and engaged with a number of parties, but ultimately Ken was the right guy for us to be in business with for the long-term. We agreed to give him majority control and positioning of the company.

It was clear to me that Ken was a commercially pragmatic person and I just felt that he was the right investor for us. It was clear to me that he was excited by what we were doing and he saw the potential in it. He told me that he actually had a dream before he decided to invest. The dream was about the company, that we were very successful, and had projects all over the world. I believe with a high degree of confidence that his dream will become a reality. I've had the same vision for years and pushed this company very hard in the last six years. It's been a real testament to perseverance and determination. It's been hard work that has taken us to where we are.

It's also clear that Ken is a very spiritual man and that those principles guide him in his life and his approach to business. So he values attributes that inspire people: honesty, integrity, fairness, hard work, and discipline are all qualities that I see in Ken and that he expects of me. They are qualities that I aspire to as well. It's nice to have a partnership with a man who espouses those qualities.

What I learned about Ken is that with him communication is everything. It is number one. I know he is a very busy man, but I also know that a high level of communication is critical and he wants to be informed. I'm young—thirty-four years old—but I've had a pretty diverse experience and some good success in business. Even being a young guy, he trusts me, and he's respectful of my opinion, my motivation, and my strategies. There have certainly been a lot of times where Ken says this is the way it's going to be, but the vast majority of the time, I set the strategy and execute it; and Ken is fully supportive.

This is a man who has a fascinating story. He really had a significant impact over in the Nutraceutical MLM world. He has been such a significant and instrumental person. I think it's fascinating to learn the lessons that he has learned along the way. I'm not going to call it a "rags-to-riches" story because I don't know enough about his formative years, but he's a self-made man, and to me that's wonderful. When people have a concept and a dream, and they deliver on it, and in particular, they deliver on it to the level of success that he has—I think that is an astonishing accomplishment.

At the end of the day you ought to be unemotional when it comes to business, but when we have projects that make commercial sense and also have positive social impact, those projects are always a little more special. I definitely feel that Ken values opportunities where we can make a positive difference in people's lives and I value that.

RICHARD VALGARDSON

Richard built the company, Irontown Homes, which Ken currently owns.
His sons manage the day-to-day operations, so it is still in the family.

IRONTOWN HOMES HAS BEEN IN EXISTENCE SINCE the late
'70s. Boise Cascade and several other larger companies
started to build houses that could be moved. We were in the
house-moving business and were hired as sub-contractors to
move these pre-built homes. Eventually we began building
our own homes in our warehouse and moving them to the
customer's location.

When the great recession hit, we realized we had grown
too quickly in some aspects and the business suffered. We
ended up in financial trouble in 2012 and 2013 and found
that we weren't able to sustain the business because we didn't
have the resources. So essentially we had to close the doors
and look for some investors. We talked to about five or six
prospects, and Ken, of course, was one of those. He was
looking for places in which to invest. Irontown Homes had
a good history, something that had been working. The other
investors were more interested in gutting the company to see
what they could get out of it—you know, pull some money
out of it and go on to the next business.

My kids and I have been brought up in the business and
we know it inside and out. I didn't know Ken very well but
I studied his background and what he did with Nature's
Sunshine. I spoke with several people who had worked in
Nature's Sunshine and realized that Ken was really a good,

honest guy. So we felt very secure about forming a partnership with him and, essentially, that's how we got started.

Part of what set Ken apart from any of the other prospective investors was his ability to look beyond the hardcore numbers, what kind of return he would get, and how fast he would get it; he actually looked at the *people*—their strengths and abilities—and then worked with that.

Knowing that someone is trusting you to get where you want to go means you've got somebody up the chain of command that wants to see you succeed, because a lot of times in business, a lot of owners take the attitude that they can find somebody else to take your place. Ken has never had that attitude. I think he wants to develop the people in the company as much as he wants to develop the company itself. He wants to use the talent that he sees within because they've got the history in the business. But all in all, he wants to make everyone a winner.

One of the things I appreciate about Ken is the trust he puts in us and it's good to have an open working relationship with him. A lot of times when you're doing business, you go up the chain and have a tendency to get personalities involved. Sometimes what you're saying can be misconstrued. I appreciate very much is that Ken has given us an open door to talk to him.

KAM VALGARDSON

Kam is the Operations Manager at Irontown Homes.

W E NEEDED TO FIND SOMEONE with a vision to protect the legacy our father is leaving us with Irontown Homes which he began thirty years ago. Because of the downturn in the market, it wasn't a simple matter of us just continuing the business. We needed someone like Ken who was excited and committed to growing the business, rather than doing what so many other investors do and just flipping businesses.

Ken's not going to buy and flip—you know, get a profit and sell it off to the next highest bidder. His intention is to run long-term. This was important to us because we were looking for stability in our lives, too. But we really wanted to see what our dad built over the last thirty years to live on. So when Kyle and Ken saw that and appreciated it, then believed in us enough to buy it, to become the owner, and take that role, and see this legacy through—for us it was great.

It's a really personal thing. It's not just business. It's not just a job. It's our father's legacy and it's something that we feel really fortunate to be a part of. Because we talked to other investors at the time, and many of them wanted to get in and out, change the model, change the name, and do all of those things. Ken didn't do that. He recognized the legacy aspect of it and stuck with us.

One thing we like about having Ken in the "owner's chair" is that he's had successful businesses in several different industries, primarily in supplements. But he also owns Lehi Roller Mills. And he's been involved in a lot of real estate transactions and multiple transactions that we've just heard bits of. But he's shown that he's got a lot of interest in a wide variety of businesses.

We haven't had major changes with Ken. He's been providing direction and resources, and we've been running pretty well. We've grown quite a bit. We started with four employees a year and a half ago when Ken came on board, and I think that we're up to about fifteen right now.

This has been an adjustment for our dad, but the nice thing is that Ken's encouraged him to be involved as much as he can. Ken recognizes that even though Irontown did face a big down-turn, he understands that those decisions that were made are not the whole story. There's forty years of work there. Ken recognizes a lot of value and experience in our dad, which is important to us. He hasn't just thrown him away and said, "We'll do this my way now."

My experience with Ken is that he's very quick to get to the point. He makes decisions quickly. He measures it, he weighs it, and he doesn't mess around. Once he makes a decision, he sticks with it. I've noticed he's a bit of a maverick, too. I mean he wants to go do things, where my natural tendency is to measure and think and study and entertain different scenarios. But Ken's gotten to where he is by making some leaps. So I look at him, my role in the company, and my personal life, too and say, "What can I do to emulate what he does a little bit more?" Ken's been a good example for me.

JASON VALGARDSON

Jason is the Operations Manager for KEB Transport.

I WOULD SAY WE, KEN AND THE VALGARDSONS, have the same core values we all feel are very important in business. It was a nice transition where our viewpoint and visions meshed with his and we were able to continue to go along the same path.

It's just added a different dynamic to have Ken on board. The nice thing that he has provided to Kam and me is the opportunity to continue to run our own separate parts of the business without a lot of micromanagement. We still have accountability, but we don't have someone who's telling us how to do everything all of the time. So Ken gives us a very long leash, allowing us to have some successes and even some failures.

Kam was very spot on in that Ken's been successful in multiple industries. You do it once, you call it a fluke. You do it over and over again, and you start to gain some respect for the gentleman who's been able to have some ups and down but has consistently continued to be successful.

Ken has said, "I don't care if you make money selling Girl Scout cookies. Just go out and be successful with it. And we'll be happy to back it and do it." That kind of attitude allows someone in our position, not being an owner of a company, to almost act like an owner in the sense of saying, "Okay, now I can go out and look at these business opportunities from a different angle."

Just the other day, Ken said, "If you need a resource to make the company more profitable, show me how you can do it, and then go do it." And that shows he instills a lot of trust in us; he feels that we have had success in different areas to be in the position that we are. And then he wants us to just continue to build on it. You're not always going to hit home runs, but you still feel comfortable swinging. That's the important part.

We would sit down with Ken and put together a plan. We'd look at it month by month and quarter by quarter and say, "For what's coming up, we would like to have X, Y, and Z to be able to hit this next level. And this is why we feel it can be successful." And he'd say, "Well, all right, go ahead and do it." Then he turns and puts the onus back on Kam and me to actually do it. That's smart because it empowers us. But it also gives us the opportunity to succeed or fail based on our own work or efforts.

Blake Larsen, a former colleague of Ken's, told me, "If Ken Brailsford is willing to go ahead and get involved with Irontown, that's a huge acumen for you, because he has an instinctive nose for business. He's very smart. He succeeds much more than he fails. And he really believes you and your family will be able to pull this off."

MICHAEL HERSHBERGER

Michael is currently the VP of Information Technology for Zija International.

KEN HAS A SOFT HEART AND CARES ABOUT PEOPLE and helping them help themselves. I admire that. He helps people out and gives them jobs and opportunities. Ken is what you see on the surface. He knows his stuff. He doesn't want to waste time. But he cares about people.

I didn't expect to see much of a human side to him. How do you separate your business personality from your human side? Ken cares deeply about his friends and family and people he doesn't even know. When he's in the office, he doesn't care as much about business as he cares about integrity. Sometimes he can seem cold and hard, sometimes even a little mean, but he's not. When we talk business, feelings don't get into it.

Ken's foundation is all about God and Jesus Christ. That's the bottom line. Then it goes to his family. It's about helping them and growing with them. Then it's business. His integrity goes over into the business. Those are the three things that shape him. He's an honest man, he's a religious man, he cares deeply about his family, and he cares about his companies. If he met Jesus Christ today, he would be able to tell him he's an honest man.

I think we all need heroes. We need to hear about people who don't cheat others and succeed. You don't have to be two-faced. You can succeed and be a good person. You don't have to rip people off to succeed. I want to emulate that and show others that there are people out there like that. No cheating, no lying, no stealing.

I admire people who have failed but learned and turned it around to make things right. What do you learn if you've never made a mistake? I respect people who make mistakes, move on, and then do the right thing from then on. There's nobody who is perfect. There are skeletons in everyone's closets. I don't expect Ken to be perfect. But I look at him and see him always striving to do the right thing.

MITCH DAVIS

Mitch is a screenwriter, film director, and film producer. Ken was involved with *The Other Side of Heaven* as an investor and is the Executive Producer of *Christmas Eve* (release date December 4, 2015), another film he has done with Mitch.

I FIRST WORKED WITH KEN fifteen years ago on my first movie project, *The Other Side Of Heaven*. I was looking for funding to produce and distribute that movie. A friend of a friend recommended I get in touch with Ken. I met with him a few times in his office, and he generously invested in that project. And I think he was happy with the results. It wasn't a positive result financially in the short term, but it ended up being a good investment for him over the long haul and people are still buying the DVDs.

In spite of the fact that he didn't make a ton of money with me the very first time we got involved fifteen years ago, he was still having a positive experience on the project. That was one of the lessons I learned from Ken; not all returns in life or in business are strictly financial. There are other kinds of returns on investments in life, so in spite of the fact that I didn't make a bunch of money right away, we maintained our friendship and our relationship, and fifteen years after the first movie, we made a second one together.

At the time we were working on *The Other Side of Heaven*, a few members of Ken's family had sort of left their faith behind and were not active in pursuing the religion of Ken and Linda. But I've been told that after viewing the movie, a couple of them had a change of heart, and the movie had a profound influence for good in their lives. It was probably the most personal experience they had with the inherent goodness of that film's ability to affect change in people's lives.

Christmas Eve is a movie we've just finished, originally called *Stuck*. It's the story of six different groups of New Yorkers who get stuck inside elevators overnight. I was impressed with how much Ken knew about movies. It was clear he'd been reading about them for years and knew all the right questions. He wasn't a slouch. He'd done his homework.

The first time I took the movie to Ken, he liked the concept, but the price tag was too high. He just said, "You know I can't take that big of a risk. Come back to me if you can figure out a way to make that same movie for a lot less money." It took me two years, but I discovered that I could make the movie in Bulgaria for literally half as much money. At that point Ken said, "Let's do it."

I learned discipline from Ken Brailsford. I could tell he really wanted to make this movie. He liked the scope of it, the feeling of it, and the lessons it teaches—the message of the movie. But in spite of his emotional attachment to the material and to me personally as a friend, he had discipline. When the price tag wasn't right he said, "I have to pass." So he threw down the gauntlet to me to go find a way to do it for a lot less money, which I did.

Ken is a loyal friend, a wise mentor and steward. It would be easy to be a loyal friend and just open your wallet and never teach anybody anything. But Ken is more like the man who would teach a man to fish, rather than buy him a fish, or give him one. He might buy you a fishing rod, and the line, hook, and bait, but then he's going to teach you how to fish.

He's the best partner I've ever had. I've had a number of partners in the movie business but never one as trusting and generous as Ken. Once he decides that he is your partner, he'll check in and ask for an accounting. But when you gain his trust, you have his trust. He's given me a lot of freedom and a lot of responsibility to make wise choices.

He allows me to fly free but periodically I get a phone call. "Mitch, I haven't heard from you in a while. What's going on?" And I better have the answers! Assuming I have the answers, he takes the good news and the bad. He's been in business long enough to know that there is always opposition and obstacles, but those can be overcome with determination and time and skill.

Ken is a very empowering leader. He is not the guy who wants all the glory. If you'll excuse the comparison, he's the Wizard of Oz behind the curtain. He doesn't have to be in front of the curtain with the bright lights on him. He's behind the curtain pulling all the levers and creating the environment in which other people can succeed. The part of that metaphor that doesn't work is that the Wizard of Oz was just a magician, a hoaxster; it may be a better comparison for me to say Ken is the puppet master. He's not the guy on stage taking all the applause. He's the guy behind the scenes making everything happen, making everything possible.

Ken reminds me of Robert Duvall, but only the best parts of him, because Duvall can be kind of irascible. What I love about Robert Duvall is his integrity—he's a straight shooter. The characters he typically plays tend to be very strong and have a lot of integrity—straight shooters. That applies to Ken, too. Duvall often plays characters that are kind of grouchy as well, but does not apply to Ken. He's a cheerful guy. It's been fun. I've been working non-stop for eighteen months on this movie and I can tell when Ken is excited because he can tell that I'm excited; and when I'm working hard, I can tell that he's grateful I'm working hard.

I also get sympathy from him once in a while. There have been a couple times when Ken has said "You sound tired, are you okay? Are you working too hard? You need to get some rest." And, in fact, I had an accident a few months ago. I broke my ankle and had to have surgery. I was calling Ken to apologize for being laid up for a little while and he said, "Oh, you probably need to rest anyway." It's great to have a boss who cares if you're getting some sleep!

I can think of no better example of the American Dream than Ken Brailsford. He is a huge success in his home, in his business, and in his religious life. He's achieved success with balance and that's extraordinary. I would call him a Renaissance man but I don't know if he can write poetry or oil paint.

It's hard to imagine Ken without envisioning Linda by his side. What those two have accomplished, they've accomplished together. And one of the reasons Ken has succeeded in such a balanced way is because he's married to a woman who expects that of him and who assists him in accomplishing that goal.

Ken's not afraid to take risks. There's probably no riskier proposition in the world than investing in an independent motion picture or an independent feature film. The battlefield is littered with the corpses who have tried to succeed in that arena and failed.

MICHAEL DANCY

Michael is VP of Alpine Air. He resides in Park City, Utah.

IT WAS PROBABLY EIGHT O'CLOCK at night when I went up and met with Ken in his living room to discuss his possible involvement in Alpine Air. He said, "I've heard a little bit about the business, tell me a little bit more."

It became very clear to me that it was much more about a personal relationship—the numbers were important, the business was important, clearly—but it was much more about a handshake and a discussion and a nose-to-nose conversation than it was, "Well, give me all the due diligence and show me the data room and all of those kinds of things." That was certainly to come, but it wasn't the purpose of the meeting.

Ken's approach was unusual to me; it was refreshing. I also felt that it was important to have a business partner who I got along with. It was more than just the numbers to me.

This was an investment that was very close to my heart. My background was with aeronautical engineering. I spent a dozen or more years with McDonnell Douglas and Boeing and I've been flying since I was about eighteen or nineteen. So this was an investment I put into this company years prior and over the years. I knew the company and knew it well. I was planning on taking an active role in the company on a post-transaction basis, so I wanted a partner I could get along with and with whom I could work well. It was about the numbers, too, but at some point, it was going to be about building the company and having a future.

I felt really comfortable about that, so after we chatted for about an hour or two, Ken said, "You know what, this is a project I think I really like. I'm in. I'll be down to your office tomorrow morning."

I thought, "Well, that's kind of strange." And that *was* very strange. You don't get somebody who says, "I'll write you a check tomorrow," and that's how it goes. It never happens that way. It wasn't like he was writing a check for the whole amount, but it certainly was a good portion that he was going to put in. It was good-faith capital, basically.

So it actually caused me to question, to sit back and think, "Who *is* this person?" I started looking into some more of the details. The person behind the person. He had done a deal with another colleague of mine several years in the past.

It was a man I've known for ten years or so. He's a very experienced individual and a principal in a very substantial private equity group in New York, quite entrepreneurial himself—so he's someone I seek counsel with from time to time—and he had actually done a deal with Ken. So the friend said, "Listen, I did a deal with Ken and it went really well. I ended up not making nearly the amount of money I thought I was going to make, so I actually went to Ken and said, 'Hey, you know I worked really hard on this project, what are your thoughts?' And Ken said, 'You're absolutely right,' and wrote me a check. He wasn't obliged to, didn't have to, there was nothing legally requiring him to do it—it was just the right thing to do."

My friend continued, "Here's the deal. He's going to hold your toes to the fire. He's going to make you do what you say you're going to do. He's going to make sure that you're following the steps and you're acting appropriately along the way. But if you do that, he's an extremely fair and generous individual."

I thought, "Now that's the kind of guy I want to do this deal with." So the situation with Ken was pretty comfortable to begin with. He has a team that helps everything to progress along—step one, step two, step three—and it seemed to me that my normal pace is much slower than Ken's normal pace. Consequently we were doing our normal due diligence on the company and the background checks and all the things we needed to do, then it came close to the end where we were getting ready to start the closing documents when it became fast and furious. So nothing was happening, then everything was happening all at once! That took some getting used to, but it was fantastic in the end. We had a completely professional office.

I remember what my colleague said, "He's going to hold

your feet to the fire, and if you do what you said you're going to do, he's going to be very generous." Well, I feel that. I feel his support. There have been times with personnel issues. As any new transaction happens, there will be personnel issues and various things that happen. And Ken, without question, would back my position and me, even though he's the majority owner, and I'm the minority, and his word goes.

That being said, I think he knows that I'm invested in this. Not just as a capital investment—but also as a personal investment. And because of that, it creates a relationship where there is no way we're going to lose. I tell that to the team all the time. I feel like Ken trusts what I'm doing. And the conversation we had in his house, and the one we had the next day, was an indication of what was to come.

Another thing—Ken trusted my opinions in a presentation to executives from the corporate offices of UPS. He and I sat together and were making the presentation. They asked my opinion and they asked Ken's opinion. Ken asked my opinion on direction of aircraft, where we're going, and specific questions about the industry.

I can say in one word what makes Ken different from others I know. And that one word is: decision. He is keen on making a decision. Right, wrong, or indifferent, he's going to make a decision. And it's almost razor blade, laser-like in terms of how he acts on that decision. If he decides he's going to do something, whatever that is, he acts on it immediately. You have to be prepared for that.

Ken will make a decision almost immediately. So with my team, I call it a "microwave conversation." I have to distill all the different things that are going on to really get to the quintessential point. I have to make sure he has all the right information, because I know that he will make a decision at the end of the discussion, even if it's thirty seconds. And I think, as part of a team and part of his executive staff, we have to realize we are dealing with someone who makes a quick decision. So we want to make sure the information we have is accurate—make sure it's the best cooking we can have up to that point, because he's going to decide if we need salt or pepper—and that's it.

It sharpens your focus a hundred percent. And I appreciate that. In the military, it's one of those things you're taught all the time. You have to make a decision and hopefully it's right. But at the end of the day, some decision is better than no decision at all. And subsequently there are ramifications. Honestly, I did the very same thing with my team here.

With Ken being involved in these different intangibles that he brings to the table, I don't think this company would do as well without him. No chance. That's not to say it couldn't happen—it's a good company. But in the length of time that we've owned it, he and I have done things that haven't been able to get done in the last twenty years. And as I said, it's a forty-year-old company. The company is what it is because of the founders that brought it to this point, but they were dead flat level for the last five to six years. Dead, flat level. And within that length of time, we've substantially increased the business.

One of the best qualities I've observed in Ken is he actually puts integrity above a business decision. Even though at times it might not be the right business decision, and he might be losing money, honoring his word and having integrity is more important.

I feel lucky every single day to have this opportunity to have Ken as a partner.

MATT WARNER

Matt Warner is the Executive Director of Améo Operations, which is a division of Zija International, where he helped launch their essential oils line.

I FIRST MET KEN about two years ago. I went in and met with him in his office at Zija in Lehi and spent twenty minutes with him talking about our essential oils. We had a great down-to-earth discussion about general business, essential oils, and about his philosophies and beliefs. We hit it off. He had the same values and principles which I believe are best for individual health and wellness, but also from a financial aspect and an integrity aspect. I felt very comfortable and at peace with this man and the company. I just knew it was right. In fact, it was in that fifteen minute interview that we both agreed verbally, "Let's work together. Let's make it happen." And the rest is history.

I've been in the MLM and direct sales industry for twenty-five years. I got my start at NuSkin, which now is in the top ten largest direct sales MLMs in the world. During that time I started and completed my MBA and just enjoyed life. And I had a real passion for business. Eventually I learned about essential oils and worked with them to a great extent. I felt it was time for me to move on from where I was, so this meeting with Ken just felt right.

Ken was always very supportive from the start. Sometimes there was major money to be spent. We did spend a lot to be able to do the proper research and get the infrastructure, enabling us to develop what we call the "Certi-5" grade essential oils. When we went to him and said, "Hey, Ken, we need to do these types of tests to validate that this truly is the best oil. And it's going to cost this large amount. He would always say, "Go do it. Let's get it done. We need to do the right thing." I was always impressed by that.

I was also impressed that Ken is very interested in the details. He wants to know everything because I believe he's learned through his business years that "the devil's in the details." He took time out of his very busy schedule. He was running multiple companies, but he came and spent time with us to make sure everything was done right. He personally invested hundreds and hundreds of thousands of dollars to bring this to light.

Ken knows the benefit of quality. You have to have clean rooms to make sure when you are doing your bottling that there are no foreign contaminants getting into any of the liquid or precious essential oils. So he immediately gave the green light and said, "Go get the clean rooms done. We need to have clean rooms to make sure it is the best quality oil that we can possibly have." And we took care of it. Ken came in and made sure it was done.

Ken was supportive of the travel necessary to meet with potential partners and mentors. He authorized everything immediately and I was able to get on planes and travel where I needed to. With our current efforts to enhance our technology and innovation Ken said, "Go on and get it done now. I support this. I want to get the best and have the best." He's always been very good to spend money to do the right thing without question. And he makes decisions very quickly. He doesn't take time to stew about it. He sees the data, he knows what he's looking for, and he approves things to go forward.

I've always been taught in my business dealings, in life, and school, that if there is a bottle neck, just like a Coke bottle, it's always at the top. I have found in dealing with Ken, that is not the case; he's very refreshing. Ken doesn't "bottle neck" you. You take good, well-thought out ideas or suggestions to him, and decisions are made so you can run with it. He knows that it's all about doing the right thing at the right time in a quick fashion. And he is always prepared to do that.

People are interested in learning about successful individuals. Ken obviously has been very successful throughout his whole life, his whole career. People want to learn what makes these individuals like Ken "tick." What kind of philosophies do they have in life and in family and in business? I run into people all the time and I always hear positive things mentioned about Ken, about just simple things: that he's a man of integrity, he honors his word, he's a great business man, and he cares about people.

Ken is so successful because he's passionate about a couple of things. One is his family. But he's also driven to create. He loves to be involved. He loves to grow businesses. And he loves to learn and read books. But I think he's been successful because he's been focused. He's had a passion and he's been driven to make a difference for his family and for all the people he works with. And he takes this message around the world to bless people's lives. He's service-oriented. I believe that is part of his success model. And he's willing to make good, educated decisions and run and not give up. Life is not easy, business is not easy. I think he's also been a visionary man and seen things that other people could not.

Ken has many qualities I'd like to emulate. I'd narrow it down, though, to humility and hard work. He gets up early, he stays up late, and he's always on the go, working to better his life, his family's life, and those around him who will listen, follow, and take direction. Ken is just a humble, good man, driven to make a difference in the world. He's just finished traveled a tour through the U.S. and Asia, He is driven to help people be successful everywhere. And he is building his dreams, while helping others to build bridges and dreams for other people around the world. It's just fun to see.

ROBERT AND MARYLOU HUGHES

Robert is Linda's brother and MaryLou, his wife. Robert is an employee of KEB Enterprises. They reside in Pleasant Grove, Utah.

ROBERT

The first impression I had of Ken was that I really respected him for his decision to serve in the Army. I admired him because of my four siblings and spouses, he was the only one that served in the military. I was impressed by his patriotism to his country and that he felt an obligation to serve. I was about fourteen or fifteen when he and Linda got married.

I admire Ken's compassion. He can relate to all different walks of people. He expects you to put in your day's worth of work, but he's always fair. I've seen Ken help more people than folks realize. I don't think he wants that advertised. I got into a lot of debt after Betty's death because the insurance didn't cover her last surgery. I had good credit and had maxed out my credit cards. I went to him after I married MaryLou and asked him for a loan and he was willing to loan it to me. We paid it back in full—but he didn't charge us interest. When my son, Greg, passed away, I think that Ken probably paid for his funeral, unbeknown to us—I'm assuming that he did it, but I don't know for sure.

Another thing I've learned about Ken is that he's always been willing to serve the Lord in whatever capacity because of his diligence to his covenants, keeping the commandments, and freely giving of his abundance to the church. I think the Lord has blessed him that way to be able to help others.

The other thing I admire about Ken is he is frugal. There will be at a restaurant where they'll order a dinner and split it; also in his choice of vehicles, they're very economical. He doesn't think he needs to drive a certain vehicle to look a certain way. He never cares if he looks like he's made of money. He'll enjoy some nice things and nice homes and his jet. If someone needed to go somewhere, he would offer his jet to get them there.

I've always enjoyed being around Ken. He always makes me feel good. He doesn't have any favorites. He's very loving. Four words I would use to describe Ken are: compassionate, knowledgeable, loyal, and trustworthy.

MARYLOU

It was really overwhelming when I met the whole family. They were very accepting of me. Ken was one who was quietly accepting of me. I liked sitting and visiting with him because he was filled with knowledge about so many things. It is interesting to hear his understanding about many of the gospel aspects, what he feels, what he thinks, and what he knows. He has a great knowledge of the church, business, and what's going on in the world. He's up to date. He likes to read and he loves movies.

He listens to people in the course of a conversation. That's been my experience with Ken and that's a sign of a good leader. He wants to hear from people. I've listened to him talk on the phone and he lets people talk. He doesn't just tell them what he wants. He's a very good listener.

I'm sure it wasn't like this when they were first married, but now that they're financially secure, I've laughed at how he deals with Linda about money. She would make a budget, then double it with her spending. He's never said anything. I think he knows she spends more money than she tells him about, but she's such a giving person. He doesn't keep track of what she spends, but just looks at her and shakes his head.

Ken's always appreciative of his parents and Linda's parents, our parents. Being an only child, born into this crazy family, he's accepting of all of us. I've never heard him say anything bad about any of us . . . his own family, immediate or extended.

KEN AND LINDA BRAILSFORD
On themselves . . .

Q: Tell us about your family?

LINDA: Well, Kenny was our first child. Sheri was born in the military at Fort Bragg. John came next. He was born in Utah in1973, so during Nature's Sunshine days. We had John without insurance and the government didn't help, so we just saved our money, then had him. Then came Lisa, Becky, and Steven was the last in 1980. I stayed home and enjoyed taking care of the kids. I was was very fortunate. But Ken did work long hours sometimes.

Q: Ken works hard. He enjoys work and the challenges. Linda, what was that like?

LINDA: I used to tell him, "Don't bring work home when you come home," and he didn't. He usually didn't answer the phone (we didn't have cell phone then, of course). When he was home, he was home, which was very nice.

KEN: You forgot that I used to get a lot of calls at home, so you made me change the number to an unlisted number.

LINDA: That's right! That's true because I wanted him to be home with the kids. That probably happened when we were in Springville and I had Lisa, so I had four kids—almost five—and I said, "You can't bring it home with you, I need help with the kids." And he was very good to not bring work home. And he did help with the kids.

The kids can remember this. We had the main floor and most of the kid's bedrooms were in the basement, so Ken would sit in the hall downstairs and read the newspaper or a book and put them to bed. This was so I could do dishes and laundry and keep up. He would sit down there, and if they got out of bed, he would say "What are you doing up? Go back to bed." So I loved it! He didn't care if he sat down with the newspaper or a book. That helped a lot when the kids were little.

Q: So that was in Springville, Utah?

Linda: Yes. We've gone through thick and thin. We have been affluent with money at times or had no money at times, but I'd always tell Ken, "Whatever you give me, I choose how to spend, so you know the budget." And we used to deal with cash. At one point I got a bank account and he would just put money in it, but it worked out perfectly because he knew what he was making and what was coming in the future with businesses, and it always worked out. As long as I had a dollar in my pocket, I was a happy camper. Isn't that funny? We would renegotiate about every year and I would say, "Okay, how much money will you give me a week this year?" And that always seemed to work. He would pay the bills and take care of all of that. The only time I paid everything was when he was in the military and he couldn't pay it. So I had to take over, but that's been a blessing to me because I had so many kids—a blessing to not to have to worry about money.

Q: Before Nature's Sunshine Products started up after Ken had been in the military, what happened then?

LINDA: We had no income, none—we lived in his parents' home upstairs and didn't pay rent—so Ken went back to school. That's when he went to UVU on the GI Bill and it paid tuition. He started selling real estate but hated it, even though he made money. He's always made money. I never worried about money.

KEN: I hated selling real estate because the homes were overpriced and I felt like the buyers weren't getting a fair shake. That's why I didn't like it. I only did it a few months.

LINDA: He worked for his aunt, then my aunts and uncles—I was fairly close in age to some of them, maybe eight years apart, but that's not a lot when you're married— and they would come over or we would go to their house. That's how we started the business—around a kitchen table.

Q: So what did you think about the business? Did you think it was a crazy idea?

LINDA: I loved it! It was fun! I liked people so it was fun to gather at the kitchen table stuffing capsules and have the kids running around having fun. I just thought if anyone could do it, we could.

Then we moved to Spanish Fork. We made enough money those first two years at Nature's Sunshine and were able to get a loan to buy a home. We lived two doors down from my Uncle Dick. The business was in his basement so it worked out perfectly. Ken walked to work and that's when Nature's

Sunshine exploded. We weren in Spanish Fork about a year and a half. Then we bought a home in Springville. Nature's Sunshine Products (NSP) really grew fast. It supported three families. Then all of a sudden there were thirty to forty people working there.

Q: So what did the kids think as they were starting to grow up a bit, watching their Dad and seeing his business?

LINDA: I think what helped the kids most was they saw the business, they took the product, they believed in herbs and health supplements, so they grew up that way and went to conventions. They weren't afraid of people or getting up on stage, most of them, as long as they could do it together. Ken sold NSP when the kids were still quite small. Then he started Enrich International. Kenny started to work there, once he could drive over. We still lived in Springville for awhile, so he drove back and forth and from then on, every child we had worked for Ken at one time or another. He's made them work—no privileges allowed.

Q: They didn't get the executive treatment?

LINDA: No and they believed in the work, so they loved it. They watched Enrich grow from the ground up and then they watched Zija grow, and they remembered NSP. All the kids became very business-minded. They saw their dad invest and make money, or maybe at times invest and *not* make money. But they haven't been afraid to ask him about things and a few of them have done quite well. They've learned Ken's principles as they've worked, not just his work ethic, and they've gotten that drive that Ken has. Kenny was so driven at Enrich that he became the manager of the IT department.

KEN: He was over the compensation program and could adjust it and fix it. That was a big job.

LINDA: And that's when computers were so complicated. I remember when Ken sold Enrich, Kenny stepped out of the business. Kenny was alive when Zija was founded, but didn't work there as he had another interest at the time. But his love was Zija.

KEN: Kenny was very detailed and very inquisitive. He would call up every night and ask me how the company was doing. He tracked those numbers and, in some ways, was like me in the his ability to follow numbers and understand their implications.

LINDA: Kenny would call when someone at Zija wrote pamphlets or brochures, He would edit and correct them. So we got to the point where we would send things to Kenny before we printed. Even though the marketing department was in charge of it, Ken would say, "Run it by Kenny." He was great at catching mistakes.

KEN: He would catch typographical errors or correct something if it was said wrong.

LINDA: So when Kenny died, really he was working from home correcting everything. When Ann (Pyne)brought him Ken's program, Kenny tracked who won the incentive trips, so he worked on that from home too. We kept asking him before he passed away, "When are you going to go into Zija to work?" And he said, "I'm fine working from home. Just keep sending everything over." He said, "One of these days, I'll go over there," but he liked to work at night, so it was nice for him to do it at home. He could catch anything. He is really missed because of that talent, by Ken especially. And our other two sons and sons-in-law have been able to step in and run departments and help save money in Ken's businesses.

KEN: John is over logistics at Zija and has saved the company literally millions of dollars since he's been there.

LINDA: When Steven was there, he did the same thing—saved Ken lots of money before he moved onto something else. It's just they've seen their dad do it, so they think it's easy. They do it blindly and they're capable of doing it because they have never even considered that they might not be capable. They didn't have any inhibitions because they saw their dad do it and thought it was easy, even though it wasn't. They were up to the task.

KEN: And then you have the girls. Sheri, who in a lot of ways is a lot like me, is not afraid to be the boss. Maybe that's because she's the oldest daughter, so she grew up seeing me run the companies. She worked for me as a secretary in the Enrich days, and then Human Resources at Zija for a time. She learned and wanted to do better and she had those skills. Then you look at Lisa—she's probably been the least involved in the companies because she and her husband moved to Arizona, but she's always been supportive and wanted to know what's going on, even though she couldn't work the business like the other kids could. Then you've got Becky.

LINDA: Well, go back to Lisa—she's driven. That's why she's in nursing school. She's driven like her dad. She wants to always improve her mind, always trying to think, "What do I really want to do?" Ken's given them that background of always have some kind of skill you can fall back on if you need to. I really feel like they might not have all the skills Ken has, but they're not his age either. They may get there but I really feel like it's an attribute—it was good for the kids to have a father like Ken even though he was absent a lot. They've seen his drive and his work ethic, and they've tried to emulate that because they love their dad. And they've loved what he's accomplished. Not that they want to be just like Ken, but they're not afraid to tackle anything.

KEN: They're not totally like me, but if you take bits and pieces and put them all in the kids, they have every trait that I've got and more. Becky is interesting because when she was growing up, she was so conscious of her appearance, as most girls are. If she got one pimple, it bothered her. So I could get her to take any of the herbs by saying, "This will help clear up your pimples," and she did. I had her on everything because she had so much faith in the products, and we, her parents, would suggest things to her. She's always been supportive of the businesses and even worked for a time as a secretary at KEB Enterprises between my last two MLM companies, before she was married. She has a lot of drive and leadership abilities just like all of our kids in their own way.

Look at Steven, he's got so many varied interests that he doesn't quite know what he wants to be, but everything that he sets his hand to, he's very good at. He invests in the stock market and makes a lot of money doing it, but he hardly understands the market itself. He just has that knack for making money.

LINDA: He learned that from his dad.

KEN: He learned by watching me and had his own business when he was a teenager, a concrete business. He had a partner who taught him how to make foundations, and he turned it into a business. Made a lot of money in it. So all the kids have skills—I think many of them are still being developed and are growing and coming about by being in a family that is so business-oriented, They have the desire and ability to run businesses. As they get older, these skills are becoming better.

Q: So each of your kids have worked for you at some point or another, but you're an entrepreneur and known as an entrepreneur. You just talked about Steven having his own business. How many of the other kids have gone out on their own and had their own business and pursued their own entrepreneurial adventures?

KEN: I don't see the entrepreneurial part them much, other than Steven. So I don't know if any of them have reached that point yet. Look at Sheri. She's talked about having her own business at some point and would be very good at it. So I think that takes time. I fell into being an entrepreneur kind of naturally, because of my background and my interests. Steven has a lot of interests like I did, but mine were more focused on business and he wants to learn everything—like this ham radio that he's mastered now to get his license, just because he wanted to.

Q: You're like that, too.

KEN: Yeah, but I don't want to do the ham radio!

LINDA: Steven just helped someone today. He had his ham radio on coming down American Fork canyon and someone had an accident on a bike going forty miles an hour. He stopped and because he could operate the ham radio, he was able to call the police and get the ambulance there quicker than someone driving down the canyon to get cell service to get an ambulance. Steven just told me that today and I said, "Well maybe that's why you chose to do it." I think all of our kids have learned good things from their father's example.

KEN: And their mother's example. A lot of Linda's traits I see in the children.

LINDA: But I think what's most interesting is that in any situation, our kids aren't afraid to be around people. Like at conventions; it's not so much the speaking, but they've grown up with people talking to them about products and business. They're not afraid to talk. A few of them don't like to be on the stage at all—half of them do, half of them don't. But they're not afraid to be around people and that's an attribute to represent the family so well. It's what makes me the happiest as a mother. And they really do look out for their dad's investments. John and Ryan, really all of our kids, may call Ken with questions because they're not afraid to talk to him. They're also not afraid to offer their opinions to him.

Ken will listen to them without saying, "No, no, no," and a lot of times, he's taken their advice. That makes me happy.

KEN: When I make suggestions and my kids have a different perspective than me, sometimes their perspective is correct. When you run businesses as an entrepreneur, you have to be open-minded. If any of my children have suggestions better than mine, I'll listen to them and do it. Just as in businesses, when I have employees with ideas better than mine, I'll take their advice and do it. If I were thinking, like some business owners, that I have all the answers, I'm just waiting to destroy my business. You've got to be flexible and listen to other people. They have great ideas.

Q: I want to go back to something for a moment. You have one of your sons that has an entrepreneurial spirit. He wants to explore and to learn. Sheri's shown some interest in business. If your kids were to come to you right now, and you were to encapsulate some advice about going into an entrepreneurial venture, what would you tell them?

KEN: Well, this is the advantage of being older—you can see all of the pitfalls in what you've accomplished. Before I would advise them, I would ask them some questions. What is it that you want to accomplish? What is the business and why do you think it will be successful? Do you have enough money to support it? When you start a business it's going to go in the hole for a while, so if you don't have enough money, it will destroy you.

Then you have to have persistence and patience to make

it successful—it might take years. Are you willing to learn from your mistakes and willing to lose that business because the odds are against you? I don't care if it's in MLM or it's traditional business—it's very difficult and most fail. Do you know enough about what you're doing and have you thought through the process to be successful? That way you can eliminate a lot of the downsides, but can you eliminate all of the downsides? I worry about my kids investing in things if they don't really understand them. I worry about them getting into a partnership where they have less than controlling interest because, based on my experience, almost every time I've invested in something where I didn't have controlling interest, I've lost my money. When I've had controlling interest, I almost always made money. So I always advise, if you're going to put money into a business venture, don't do it unless you have control.

So those are some of the things I would tell them. I wouldn't say yes or no, do it or don't do it, but I would tell them whether *I* would do it or not. If they were to make an investment where they weren't going to have control and I advised them not to . . . if they did it anyway, I'd say let's see how it turns out, but my guess is that it won't turn out the way they thought it would. But, then again, if they lose their money in it, they might not tell me, and it would be a learning experience. You'll never go through life and have everything work out perfectly.

Q: If they lose money, what is your approach going to be?

KEN: I would just say, "Did you learn from it so you don't make that mistake again?" And if they learn from it, then it's an expensive learning experience, just like I've had some expensive learning experiences.

LINDA: Amen to that.

KEN: That doesn't make you a failure because you have a business fail. Maybe it wasn't the right time or the right business, or you didn't have the right employees, didn't have control, or whatever, so you learn from that and eliminate those types of situations going forward. Life is about learning; we're not perfect. Do we make the same mistake twice? That's why I can tolerate an employee who makes a mistake, even if it's costly, if they own up to it, if they're loyal, and if they don't repeat it again. But if they make the same mistake again, I have to let them go because they're not willing to learn from those mistakes.

LINDA: I think the biggest things our kids have learned from Ken is they've seen their dad fail and they've seen him overcome it. I think that's the biggest lesson. I've watched them overcome things in their lives that I don't think they would have overcome if they hadn't seen their dad's example of losing everything and rebuilding it again. It's a hard thing when you go through any trials. I think that's what got us through Kenny's death, really, because we had been through other hard things but we bonded together and could see the other side of it. We could look at the good side. Even when Ken went through bankruptcy, the kids could see that he wanted to repay all of it; they also saw how hard he worked to be able to repay it. And I think that's given the kids their drive to do better in any situation, whether going back to school like Lisa, or overcoming a problem in their younger lives as teenagers. They had the persistence their dad had. I think it really did help them.

Q: Now that the kids are all grown up and you have grandkids, that can sometimes show how effective your parenting was.

LINDA: I think they're a hundred times better parents than we ever were. I really believe that. They chose the right partners. Our parenting was so hodge-podge sometimes because Ken was off doing some business, and I was here trying to do some service for the community or for our church. Then we have the kids. But our kids can see the whole picture better than Ken and I ever could. Sometimes we just thought, let's just get through this week, then we'll see where we are. But our kids are so much better than we are and what a blessing that is to us and our grandkids. I feel like they're trying to do what's right and that makes me so happy. If you can get kids through the ages of fourteen to twenty-one, amen to the parents. They've done a great job.

Q: What are some of the blessings that you can see and life lessons that you two have taught your kids and grandkids that are really starting to show?

KEN: I have to give ninety percent of the credit to Linda for raising the kids. I was absent a lot to be able to build the businesses that I had, which is not good for building a family relationship. So a lot of that burden fell on Linda. She was so loving and kind that our kids have learned how to be loving and kind, even though it's tough in some situations. Those are important things that the kids have learned in their family relationships.

LINDA: I think our family motto is, "We don't give up!" I didn't give up on Ken, he didn't give up on me, the kids didn't give up on our family, they didn't give up on their situations. We stuck together. We got through it.

KEN: I believe a large part of it is that we had God in our lives and tried to do what's right, even though I certainly failed at times with that.

LINDA: They knew they were loved and they knew that they could do anything and we would support them if they were trying to better themselves.

KEN: One thing I want to backup just a little bit on is the bankruptcy because about 1980, for whatever reason, God told me that he was going to take everything away from me. I thought I had arrived at the top of the world financially, with all the freedoms that come with having money and success, and then I had this inspiration come to me. "I'm going to take everything away from you." Over the course of the next four year, He literally took everything away from me except my family and my ability to make money to continue supporting the family.

When He told me that, as anyone who goes through bankruptcy knows, they are two choices. Either blame God and say, "Why did you do this to me?" or say, "Well, it's my own fault and I'm learning something." Many of the failures I've had in my life have been devasting in a lot of respects— not to be compared to Job in the Old Testament who lost his family and fortune—I didn't lose my family. I just lost money but the Lord has given me far more back. I attribute that success to Him because I never blamed God, nor did Linda or our children. We were able to go through that and come out stronger in every respect—spiritually, financially, everything—it took time but we were able to achieve it. We always believed that God gave us everything and He has the ability to take it away as well. It's His anyway—no one can say, "I'll never be broke again," or "I'll never do this again." You don't know. God can take anything away. He doesn't do it with malice. He does it to make us stronger—that's been my philosophy in life.

LINDA: Just to summarize, Kenny is our oldest, then Sheri, John, Lisa, Becky, and Steven. I can hardly say their names without thanking them a hundredfold for being my children because, really, when it comes down to it, we couldn't have done it without them.

KEN: Yeah, I don't think we could have achieved all these things without our children.

Q: Explain that.

KEN: Well, they're supportive. They helped the businesses, especially in their infancy. They've been loyal and, certainly in our case, they have worked hard and helped build our enterprises, so they're an integral part of our success, as most children are later in their parents' lives.

LINDA: Also who they marry has made them even better. We've got Scott, Michelle, Mark, Ryan, and Amy, and I claim them as my kids. They're part of our family, and in a sense, they've taught us almost as much as our children because they've become a real part of our family. I'm in awe because of the things they do and the people they are trying to be. No one's perfect, but anyone who really has a great love for God, their family, the world around them, and other people, would say the same things about their children and their spouses and about what family means.

KEN: And our children's spouses, and now our grand-children, are growing up, and they're contributing to the family, too—the same thing—that's part of the cycle of life. We were young once and then the children become middle-age, we get older and our children get older and have their own families. It's part of life and the intent is that every generation become better and more successful than the previous one in all ways—spiritually, financially—every possible way.

Q: Let me go back. You brought up Kenny and mentioned how difficult it was to lose him, but you also gained a lot of strength.

LINDA: We were blessed in a way when Kenny died because we had moved into the same condo building Kenny was living in for the a year and a half before he died. If we hadn't made that move, hadn't had that time to spend with him, I don't think

I would have been able to make it through his death. In those eighteen months, I felt it kind of closed a gap that I had felt with Kenny, because he was our oldest and had never married. He kind of pulled away from the family—not in a bad way, but he didn't see us as much. So that was a tender mercy we were given, to be able to live so close to him those last months of his life. I feel very blessed because if it. Also, when Kenny died, if it hadn't been for our other children and for the support they gave us, we wouldn't have made it. They were very loving and supportive, and even though our loss was so devastating, it brought us close together. We have done so many great things together as a family since then. Lisa started it—on the anniversary of Kenny's death every year, we do some type of service for someone. Lisa started. How old was Kenny when he died?

KEN: He was forty-three.

LINDA: Lisa called us and said, "We're going to do forty-four acts of service for Kenny's birthday." She divided it by six, so we each did that many acts of service that day. It was a sweet, wonderful thing. Becky had some great stories; all of the kids had great stories. Becky was in Hawaii at the time, so she went and bought a bunch of cold water, and her boys took it up and down the beach, giving it to people. Lisa was in line at a fast food place and told the cashier when she paid her money, "I want to pay for the car behind me." I was driving down the street and felt impressed to stop—this couple was sitting on their porch and I helped them. It's just little acts of service—I can't think of all of them off the top of my head, but we all did them.

Q: So are you doing it on every anniversary?

LINDA: We're trying to keep it up. I most certainly have. Some of the family haven't been as diligent as others but I can tell you Sheri goes to his grave a lot. That's a tender thing because she was close to her brother. I can always call John or Steven anytime, and they'll talk to me about Kenny, and that's wonderful. That means so much to a mother.

Q: Ken, how did Kenny's death impact or change you?

KEN: I think when you have a child die before you, it makes you think about your own mortality more, realizing that generally children should outlive their parents and not the other way around. So you think about your death and mortality more and wonder if you're doing the things that you're supposed to do so that you'll all be able to be together in the next life. Are we keeping the commandments of Heavenly Father? Are we helping other people? Are we doing everything we were sent to this Earth to do? That's how it's impacted me. The interesting thing about Kenny's death is that, as Linda said, we moved down closer to where he was living, not with that being the primary driving force. But it's one of those tender mercies of God that had us do, and once we moved there, we realized that was why we were supposed to be there. When Kenny passed, we didn't feel like we were supposed to be there anymore, so we started looking for another place. That's how we ended up in Park City.

Q: Here's one of the values in this and why I bring it up— it's a big part of your life—family is very important to you

and other people who read this may be struggling with it. They want to see how you're doing and how you handled it.

KEN: Nobody's going to go through life without challenges, and how to cope with those challenges makes a big difference when you realize that God is in control and would do nothing to hurt you in the end. Sometimes it hurts, but that's how we grow. When we struggle, have adversity, have challenges, have something hurt us, if we don't blame God but look at ourselves and see what we can learn from it, then we can come through it and we'll be stronger. We wonder, "Why did that happen to me?" Maybe not in this life, but in the next, we'll understand, and we'll be grateful to God for letting us go through it.

Q: You made a very conscientious decision and usually don't go into something where you know you're going to lose money, so why did you put up money to help produce *The Other Side of Heaven?*

KEN: *The Other Side of Heaven* was a story about a young man and his three year mission to Tonga where he had a wonderful impact on the native people. I thought that story needed to be told. When I first decided to do it, it was a $7 million total investment, not by me, but by all of the investors. I said I would invest $100,000 and told Ann (Pyne) that I didn't expect to get it back. Mitch Davis came near the end of his fundraising and said that they were $100,000 short, but because I thought the movie should be made, I said I would put up the other $100,000. So it was a $200,000 investment. Again I told Ann that I didn't expect to make my money back. To this day, I haven't received a dollar back on that investment. Would I do it all over again? Yes! Sometimes it's not about the money. But if you don't make money you can't keep helping people. However, in this particular instance, it was about helping people who were going to see the movie and its message, which could benefit their lives, make their lives better. So I was willing to throw $200,000 away and do it because I've seen the end result and I still believe it will benefit the lives of many viewers who watch it.

Q: I wanted to talk about Lehi Roller Mills and how immediately after you won the bid, another bidder approached Bart (Anthony) and said they would pay more than your bid was. You asked Bart to find out what they wanted to do with the mill. Bart found out that they wanted the land to develop and his recollection of that was you saying, "Well that's nearly thirty employees that are going to be out of work. So no, I'm not going to do that."

KEN: Well, if they had said they were going to do essentially the same thing with the business that I've done with it, then I might have taken the deal and sold it to them. But that place is a part of the community. I didn't want to displace the employees. I didn't want to tear down those historic buildings, and I didn't want to see the business destroyed. I've driven past that place for years, maybe a thousands times since living here. For a long time I had the impression as I'd drive by that I should be involved with the mill, but I didn't see how that was going to happen. Now we've got a chance to keep it going.

It's about the people first and the money second. It's always that way in my life. If it's not going to benefit people, then I won't, or I can't do it. If it's going to benefit people, then I always know that if I can benefit people's lives, the money will take care of itself. And if not, I don't view the money as my money anyway—it's God's money and He's in control.